What people are saying about …

Revise Us Again

"Perhaps you know Frank Viola as a prophetic voice lifting up
Jesus Christ and God's eternal purpose; perhaps you know him
for his iconoclastic writings on church reform. Maybe you're
encountering his work for the first time. In any case, you're in
for a compelling treat with *Revise Us Again*. In ten easy-to-read
chapters, Frank gently—but directly—invites us to revise our
long-held 'scripted' assumptions about how God communicates
to us, how Christians speak to one another, the work of the Holy
Spirit in our midst today, and the content of the good news we
proclaim to our friends and neighbors. The result is vintage
Viola—a sacred-cow barbecue with little aftertaste. Highly
recommended!"

Mike Morrell, journalist and
futurist, zoecarnate.com

"Frank masterfully describes the process of success for our future
as Christ followers, and God is writing us a prescription in this
book. His prescript for us is to de-script us from religious mind-
sets and activities that do not profit us or others—and to rescript
us into His heart, His ways, and His likeness. Frank takes us to the
core issues of the heart and of life in Christ. Take the prescription

by reading this book, and you will go forward in a mind-set that is healthy and whole for your journey ahead."

Robert Ricciardelli, founder of
Converging Zone Network and
Visionary Advancement Strategies

"I loved this book. I wish I would have written it myself. From the introduction to the concluding remarks, there was a spirit of grace that invited me to reexamine some of my own ideas about the Christian life. While *Revise Us Again* is an easy read, its message is profound! Please give yourself permission to ask some hard questions. I highly recommend Frank's new book."

S. J. Hill, Bible teacher, speaker, and author
of several books, including *Enjoying God*

"I like short books. They're usually written from pure motives. Frank Viola's *Revise Us Again* is not only short but full of humor and wisdom—a plea (with directions!) for sanity in the storm of flesh-corrupted chaos that is called 'Christianity' in the twenty-first century."

Don Francisco, songwriter and recording artist

What people are saying about …

From Eternity to Here

"*From Eternity to Here* is a masterpiece. A must read for those who believe and for others who want to believe. It reads like a movie on paper."

Dr. Myles Munroe, pastor and author of
Rediscovering the Kingdom and *God's Big Idea*

"Frank continues to challenge the church-at-large with a powerful mind, an impassioned voice, and a love for the bride of Christ. You need to get this book and wrestle with Frank through the biblical passages regarding our identity in Christ as His body and the mission our God has entrusted to us."

Ed Stetzer, author of *Breaking the Missional Code,* www.edstetzer.com

"As Viola unfolds the glorious story of God's quest for a bride, readers will find their imaginations inspired and their lives transformed. The sheer beauty of God's magnificent plan compels our allegiance and revolutionizes our lives. This retelling of the 'old, old story' is a much-needed gift to the church today."

Greg Boyd, pastor, theologian, and author of *Letters from a Skeptic, Myth of a Christian Nation,* and *God at War*

What people are saying about …

Reimagining Church

"In *Reimagining Church*, Frank Viola is at the top of his game, showing a serene, soaring mastery of the theology of church as organism rather than organization."

Leonard Sweet, author of *Soul Tsunami, 11*, and *So Beautiful*

"Dissent is a gift to the church. It is the imagination of the prophets that continually calls us back to our identity as the peculiar people of God. May Viola's words challenge us to become the change that we want to see in the church … and not to settle for anything less than God's dream for Her."

Shane Claiborne, author of *The Irresistible Revolution*, activist, and recovering sinner (thesimpleway.org)

"True to form, this book contains a thoroughly consistent critique of prevailing forms of church. However, in *Reimagining Church*, Frank Viola also presents a positive vision of what the church can become if we truly reembraced more organic, and less institutional, forms of church. This is a no-holds-barred prophetic vision for the church in the twenty-first century."

Alan Hirsch, author of *The Forgotten Ways* and *The Shaping of Things to Come*

REVISE US AGAIN

LIVING FROM A CHRISTIAN SCRIPT
renewed

FRANK VIOLA

transforming lives together

REVISE US AGAIN
Published by David C. Cook
4050 Lee Vance View
Colorado Springs, CO 80918 U.S.A.

David C. Cook Distribution Canada
55 Woodslee Avenue, Paris, Ontario, Canada N3L 3E5

David C. Cook U.K., Kingsway Communications
Eastbourne, East Sussex BN23 6NT, England

David C. Cook and the graphic circle C logo
are registered trademarks of Cook Communications Ministries.

The Web site addresses recommended throughout this book are offered as a
resource to you. These Web sites are not intended in any way to be or imply an
endorsement on the part of David C. Cook, nor do we vouch for their content.

LCCN 2010923215
Hardcover ISBN 978-1-4347-6865-0
International Trade Paperback Edition ISBN 978-1-4347-0101-5
eISBN 978-1-4347-0331-6

© 2010 Frank Viola
Published in association with the literary agency of Daniel Literary
Group, 1701 Kingsbury Dr., Ste. 100, Nashville, TN 37215

The Team: John Blase, Sarah Schultz, Jack Campbell, Karen Athen
Cover Design: Amy Kiechlin
Cover Photo: iStockphoto

Printed in the United States of America
First Edition 2010

1 2 3 4 5 6 7 8 9 10

011411

CONTENTS

Introduction

The very day I was converted to Christ, I was handed a script. And I began living from it.

Over the years, that script has expanded both in size and variety. As I attached myself to various churches, denominations, parachurch organizations, and ministries, new lines of text were added to my script.

In the same way, every human being is scripted through their upbringing, their surroundings, their culture, and their religious influences. Our scripting works unconsciously. We are usually unaware when the scripting is happening to us. Somewhere along the line, however, I became aware of the religious script that was given to me.

As Christians, we can safely assume that some of the script we have been handed matches the heart and mind of our Master. But typically, much of it doesn't.

In such cases, we want those lines of script that are incompatible with the teachings of Jesus *revised* and *re-visioned* to match His heart and mind.

Transformation (spiritual formation) can be described as editing out that which is not Christ and revising that which is. Or to use Paul's metaphor in Ephesians, it's a matter of "putting off the old" and "putting on the new."

Revising is a process. And it begins with opening ourselves up to the possibility that the script we have been given in life is not perfect. It's in need of regular evaluation and reevaluation.

In the pages that follow, I will introduce you to ten specific areas where many of us are in need of revising. Some of these areas touch on things that are rarely talked about in Christian circles today. They work below the surface. Yet once they are exposed, we can look back and say to ourselves, "How did I miss that?" (This has been my experience at least.)

A good bit of what you will read in this book will be intuitive. Therefore, I expect that during the course of your reading, you will say in your heart, "But of course!"

In much of this, I'm simply sharing some of the discoveries I've made in my own personal struggles and challenges as a follower of Jesus Christ. So I hope you will find this book to be challenging, inspiring, and encouraging all at the same time.

My hope is that the Holy Spirit of God, who writes not on tablets of stone but on the tablets of our hearts, will use this book to help edit those religious habits that do not map to His heart, and in turn, begin rescripting us into the glorious image of Christ.

CHAPTER 1

GOD'S THREE-FOLD SPEAKING

REVISING THE LORD'S VOICE

There's a very obscure passage in the Old Testament that sheds light on how God communicates His mind to His people. It's found in Jeremiah 18:18:

> *The teaching of the law by the priest will not be lost,*
> *nor will counsel from the wise, nor the word from*
> *the prophets.*

The ancient Hebrews divided the Old Testament up into three sections. The first section is called the Torah, or the Law. It includes the first five books of the Bible. The steward of the Torah is the priest.

The second section of the Old Testament is the Prophets. It includes the Major and Minor Prophets and the Historical Books. The steward of the Prophets is, of course, the prophet.

The third division of the Old Testament is called the Wisdom Literature, or "the Writings." It includes Psalms, Ecclesiastes, Proverbs, Job, and the Song of Solomon. The steward of the Wisdom Literature is the sage, or wise man.

These three sections of the Old Testament represent the three major ways in which God communicates His mind to His people.

Where We've Been

One of the greatest obstacles to hearing the Lord's voice is our religious background. Virtually every Christian has at some point been given a narrow lens through which he or she interprets Scripture, the Lord, and the Lord's speaking.

Therefore, it's critical that we understand that we all have been given such a lens. The following list shows how incredibly powerful our religious backgrounds are in shaping these lenses.[1] The list is obviously tongue in cheek, but I believe the truth is not far off.

Suppose that you are traveling to work and you come to a stop sign. What do you do? Well, that depends on your religious background. For example ...

1. A fundamentalist, taking the text very literally, stops at the stop sign and waits for it to tell him to go.

2. A Christian who follows the traditions of his denomination does not bother to read the sign, but she will stop if the car in front of her does.

3. A seminary-educated evangelical preacher might look up *stop* in his English lexicon and discover that it can mean (1) something that prevents motion or (2) a location where a train or bus lets off passengers. The main point of his sermon the following Sunday on this text is this: When you see a stop sign, realize that it is a place where traffic is naturally clogged; therefore, it's a good place to let off passengers from your car.

4. A legalist does one of two things. She takes another route to work that does not have a stop sign so she doesn't run the risk of disobeying the law. Or she may stop at the stop sign and pray, "Thank You, oh Lord, for Your commandment to stop." She waits three seconds according to her watch and then proceeds. She also keeps a condemning eye out to see if others run the stop sign.

5. A New Testament scholar notices that there is no stop sign on Mark Street, but there is one on Matthew Street and Luke Street. He then concludes that the ones on Luke and Matthew Streets were copied from a sign on the street that no one has ever seen called "Q" Street.[2]

6. A prophetic preacher of end-time theology notices that the square root of the sum of the numeric representations of the letters S-T-O-P (which are *sigma tau omicron pi* in the Greek alphabet) multiplied by 40 (the number of testing), and then divided by 4 (the number of the earth) equals 666. Therefore, she concludes that stop signs are the dreaded mark of the beast, a harbinger of divine judgment, and must be avoided at all costs.

7. A Charismatic/Pentecostal will stop only if he feels led of the Spirit and the sign is a *rhema* word and not a *logos* word.

8. A prosperity preacher will stop at the sign, make a positive confession about stopping, and offer "the prayer of Jabez," concluding that God must make her rich.

9. An Arminian believes that if he runs the stop sign he will lose his salvation. So with fear and trembling, he works hard at stopping at every stop sign.

10. A Calvinist believes that God has predestinated her reaction to the sign. If she runs the stop sign, she was never saved to begin with. If she stops, she was elected before creation.

11. A Southern Baptist believes that God wants him to stop at the sign, but he will still be saved if he does not. For if you once stopped, you have always stopped.

12. Upon seeing the stop sign, a libertine begins to sing, "Hallelujah, I'm free," pushes her foot down on the pedal, and runs the stop sign at full throttle. She then gets run over by a Mack truck.

13. A liberation theologian believes that stop signs should stop only those who are of the elitist, wealthy class. But the poor are free to run them whenever they wish.

Silly, yes, but this list makes a point. We all have a lens that we inherited from our religious background. And we are conditioned to interpret Scripture, the Lord, and His speaking through that lens.

How God Communicates His Mind

The Torah contains the foundations on which the community of God's people are built. The Torah includes God's enduring moral principles—the standards that spring from His very nature. These standards do not change, nor can they be compromised. In the Old Testament economy, the priest was the person who taught the Torah.

The Prophets section of the Bible often seems to contradict the Torah. The prophet is the person who enters the community of God's people and causes an abrasive, disruptive upheaval of what the community believes or practices.

The prophet challenges the people's *response* to the Torah, which is often a legalistic or libertine response.

In reality though, the prophet really doesn't contradict the Torah. He contradicts the people's response to it. We are fallen creatures, and we sometimes turn the standards of God into dead rituals. At other times we misapply or disregard them altogether. The prophet is needed at such times.

The Wisdom Literature contains something that we Christians often do not have a great abundance of—wisdom. Wisdom is knowledge gained through experience. It also includes a predictive element.

Because of his long experience, a wise person can detect patterns. And he's able to foresee outcomes (Luke 11:49; Prov. 22:3).

A wise person may make a statement like this: "What you just said sounds really good, but it's not going to work, and here's why …"

The instrument of the Wisdom Literature is the sage, the wise old man with the gray head. The sage is sought after for his wisdom because he has the experience of life. As a result, he can peer into the future.

The priest is authorized by the authority of the Torah, which contains what God has *previously spoken*. The prophet is authorized by the *present burden* of the Lord that the Holy Spirit lays upon him. The sage is authorized by his experience and the fruit of his wisdom, which can be evaluated by the *future outcome* of his counsel (Luke 7:35).

Put another way, the priest looks to *the past* and asks, "Is this scriptural? Is this right?"

The prophet looks to *the present* and asks, "What is God saying to us right now? What is His present leading?"

The sage looks to *the future* and asks, "How will our present actions affect the future? Is this decision wise or foolish?"

To put it in the language of the Bible: The priest asks, "What do these stones mean?" (Josh. 4:6). The prophet asks, "Is there any word from the LORD?" (Jer. 37:17). And the sage asks, "Where can wisdom be found?" (Job 28:12).[3]

The Inherent Dangers of Each

Each form of God's speaking has its own dangers if not attended to by the other forms. If a church is conditioned to recognize the Lord's will through only the form of Torah, it will become ritualistic at best or judgmental, self-righteous, and legalistic at worst. It will need the prophetic word as well as the word of wisdom to balance it.

A church that recognizes the Lord's speaking via only the lens of the prophet will be unstable and erratic at best. At worst, it will be deceived. This is because a prophet's revelation can be bogus. Thus, a prophetic word should be tested by its faithfulness to what God has already said (i.e., Torah) and by its future outcome (i.e., wisdom).

If a church recognizes the Lord's will through only the lens of wisdom, it will be given over to human reasoning and empty philosophy. True wisdom will always be faithful to what God has already said (i.e., Torah), and it will be responsive to the inbreaking of an authentic prophetic word.

Consequently, we should embrace all three forms because God speaks through each.

Unfortunately, our religious backgrounds condition us to recognize the Lord's voice through only one form. Those who have a fundamentalist background tend to recognize the Lord speaking through only the Torah. Guidance must contain a standard or principle of God, which usually has a chapter and verse attached to it. But this narrow lens blinds them from recognizing God's guidance through the other modes.

Those who come from a Charismatic/Pentecostal background tend to recognize the Lord's voice through only the prophetic word. It must be peppered with, "I sense the Lord saying" … "I have a word from God" … "The Lord showed me" … "Thus saith the Lord." Appeals to Scripture or wisdom have very little registration.

Those from mainline denominations tend to recognize God speaking through whatever sounds reasonable. Wisdom is their language. What God has said in the past often carries little weight. And prophetic revelation is suspect.

Put differently, those who prefer Torah-speaking are *thinkers*. Those who prefer prophetic-speaking are *feelers*. And those who prefer wisdom-speaking are *doers*. Three temperaments, three denominations, and three forms of God's speaking.

It's worth noting that our temperament is connected to our religious background. We are typically drawn to the denomination or movement that matches our disposition. Doers tend to gravitate toward denominations like Baptist. Feelers tend to gravitate toward the Charismatic/Pentecostal Movement. And thinkers tend to gravitate toward fundamentalist denominations, Presbyterian, or Anglican churches. Parachurch organizations and many large movements usually combine two of these temperaments, typically thinkers and doers or feelers and doers. I admit these are generalizations; however, I believe they are very close to reality.

Whether we realize it or not, our religious background is a major hurdle that stands in the way of laying hold of the mind of Christ individually and corporately.

Accordingly, God in Christ by the Spirit discloses His will through *all* three modes.

The Mind of Christ

In 1 Corinthians 12:1–2 (NKJV), Paul writes:

> *Now concerning spiritual gifts, brethren, I do not want you to be ignorant: You know that you were Gentiles, carried away to these dumb idols, however you were led.*

Notice that Paul mentions "dumb idols." What exactly is a dumb idol? It's not an idol with a low IQ. A dumb idol is an idol that doesn't have the power of speech. It's a mute idol.

Before the Corinthian believers came to Christ, they were following pagan gods that didn't possess the power of speech. These gods were mute. They were dumb. Paul goes on, saying the following (this is my paraphrase of verses 3–6):

> *Remember how you served mute idols? Well, now you serve a God who speaks, and He speaks through you and your fellow members of the body of Christ. For example, when you say, "Jesus is Lord," God's own Spirit is speaking through you. There are varieties of spiritual gifts, but it's the same Spirit. There are varieties of ministries, but it's the same Lord. And there are varieties of effects, but it's the same God who is working through them all. The one true God speaks through a variety of different ways via His one body.*

Notice that God communicates in a variety of ways, but it's the same God who is doing all the speaking. And God does that speaking through His body, i.e., a local assembly that allows Him to speak through its members.

Consequently, the mind of God can only be made fully known through a corporate body of believers.

Jesus Christ has the power of speech. He's not a dumb idol. And when He speaks, He reveals the mind of God. But Christ never reveals His whole mind through an individual. It takes a body of believers to lay hold of His mind together.

Hence, Paul says in 1 Corinthians 2:9–10:

> *However, as it is written: "No eye has seen, no ear has heard, no mind has conceived what God has prepared for those who love him"—but God has revealed it to us by his Spirit. The Spirit searches all things, even the deep things of God.*

Consider the following words:

> *Eye has not seen.* He's speaking of a single eye. A solo eye has not seen.

> *Ear has not heard.* An individual ear has not heard.

> *And it has not entered into the heart of man.* A single heart hasn't received.

Now listen to Paul in 1 Corinthians 2:16 (NKJV):

> For "who has known the mind of the LORD that he
> may instruct Him?"

This is an absurd question. But notice the singular: "Who has known the mind of the Lord that he [singular] may instruct him?"

The answer is obvious. No individual has God's mind. But then Paul makes this remarkable statement: "But we [plural] have the mind of Christ." We, corporately—as His body—possess the mind of Christ. Incredible.

The mind of Christ is discoverable. Jesus Christ is not a dumb idol. He has the power of speech. He desires to speak and reveal His thoughts. But the mind of Christ is a corporate discovery. It's a corporate pursuit. It's not the property of any individual. It's the property of the body of Christ working together to secure it.

As a result, all three ways of God's speaking in Christ (Torah, prophetic, and wisdom) should be held in tension. The reason? Jesus Christ incarnates all three modes.

> Jesus Christ is the real Priest as well as the Torah itself.

> Jesus Christ is the real Prophet as well as the Prophetic Word.

> Jesus Christ is the real Sage as well as Wisdom itself.

Our Lord reveals His will to and through a local community of believers when they are seeking to lay hold of His mind together. The local assembly is the vehicle that God has chosen to disclose His mind. Through some believers, He speaks as Prophet. Through others, He speaks as Priest. Still through others, He speaks as Sage.

The speaking may sound different, but it's the same Christ working through each one.

The Lord helps us to revise our ears so that we may learn to hear the voice of the Shepherd through each one of His sheep.

CHAPTER 2

THE LORD TOLD ME

REVISING CHRISTIANEZE

In a number of movements in the Christian faith, God's people are taught by both precept and example to preface many of their decisions with the words "God told me."

> "God told me to start attending Pastor Fielding's church."

> "God told me to marry Felicia Norris."

"God told me to buy a Mercedes."

"God told me that I'm a prophetess."

"God told me to break up with Rotunda."

"God spoke to me and told me to rebuke my aunt
Nina."

God told me … it's central to the vocabulary of a number of
Christian traditions.

Several years ago, I made a disturbing observation about this
type of language. That in well over half the cases when I've heard
a person use the words "God told me," what they said later turned
out to be what the person wanted, and God got the rap for it.

Before you read on, please keep in mind that I believe that God
speaks to His people in a variety of different ways. So this chapter
doesn't question whether or not God speaks to His children. He
certainly does. What I'm addressing here is the tendency of many
Christians to announce that God has told them something.

Some Illustrations

A Christian woman I had known for many years represents what I've
observed innumerable times with innumerable people. We'll call her

Sally. Sally would routinely preface her decisions this way. "God is telling me to homeschool my kids." "God is telling me to begin giving one hundred dollars each month to Apostle Chestwald's worldwide ministry." "God told me to purchase a used Toyota Camry."

In virtually every case, Sally would end up not following through on what God told her to do. Oftentimes, it would only be a few weeks later.

She stopped homeschooling her kids. When someone asked her about this, she said, "Well, it's really not for me. I think God wants me to send them to private school."

Hmmm ... did God change His mind that quickly?

When asked why she didn't buy the car that "God told" her to buy, she said, "It has some problems with it that I don't want to inherit. Plus, we can't afford it right now anyway. I'm feeling led to lease a car instead."

Hmmm ... God changed His mind again.

Not long ago I was talking to a friend who has a network of churches he's in relationship with. In conversing over some issues, I recommended to my friend that he invite one of my coworkers to spend a weekend with his network, as I believed it would be a great help to them. His first response was, "Yes, sure."

A few days later, I thanked him for being open to inviting my coworker. He then replied, "Actually, I sense that God is telling me to wait and to take it slow."

Those words short-circuited all conversation on the matter.

If God spoke, what else could be said? That's quite the trump card.

He hasn't invited my coworker to visit his network, and I doubt he ever will.

My friend's response is very common in these circumstances. And in most cases like this, what it really means is: "I don't feel comfortable doing this. I'm afraid to expose *my* people to someone other than me. So I've changed my mind."

Here's another one that's a close cousin to "God told me."

"I'm so sick. I can't endure this pain. Why is God doing this to me?"

Hmmm … God is picking on you because you are sick? Is your pain really His fault?

Or how about this one:

"Pastor Melvin announced this past Sunday that as a result of our church's vow to tithe on our gross last year, God provided the money to build our new one-hundred-million-dollar church building. Isn't God good!?"

Ummm … really? God is good because your church tithed to buy a very expensive building?

Point: I've routinely watched God get credit for things that He never authored and blamed for things He never imagined.

I wonder how the Lord feels when this happens.

What's Really Behind It?

All of this has led me to ask a simple question: "Why do so many people feel the need to broadcast to others what they think God told them?"

I'm loathe to judge the motives of others. In fact, motive-judging is one of the most destructive things that a Christian can engage in. It destroys relationships. For this reason, the Lord had some very strong thoughts about it (Matt. 7:1–5; 1 Cor. 4:3–5).

However, upon the honest admission of some Christians whom I've known, here are six reasons why at least *some* people choose to use this hyperspiritual language. Read their own confessions:

- "If I could say that 'God told me' to do something, then I didn't feel responsible for whatever He told me to do. God was responsible."

- "It made me sound more spiritual when I made sure that people knew that it was God who was talking to me. Plus, all my friends talk this way."

- "I was afraid that if I didn't say, 'God told me,' people wouldn't accept what I said. Or they would argue with my decision."

- "I had a desire to lead others. If I could convince them that God told me something, I found that they would follow me."

- "I really didn't want to keep conversing about a specific matter that I didn't feel comfortable with, so I ended it with 'God told me.' How can anyone argue with that?"

- "I wanted so bad to hear God's voice that I thought if I said that He always spoke to me in everything, it would become a reality."

Please reflect on the above. And note that these people were largely unconscious of their motives until later.

I know that there are many Christians who don't have these motives operating in them. In such cases, I believe it's a matter of thoughtlessly borrowing the language of a particular Christian subculture. "Everyone else talks that way in my church, so I guess I just naturally picked it up subconsciously."

The Testimony of the New Testament

As I read through the New Testament, I never see any Christian talking like this. Paul will sometimes quote the Lord Jesus. But in those cases, he is quoting what the Lord taught when He was on earth (e.g., Acts 20:35; 1 Cor. 7:10).

In one instance, Paul was forced to share his spiritual experiences. But when he did, he admitted that he was playing the fool in doing so (2 Cor. 12:1ff.).

Paul also told Luke (or perhaps someone else who knew Paul told Luke) about several supernatural visions he received where the Lord appeared to him and spoke to him. But those cases were clearly supernatural, and they had to do with the direction of Paul's apostolic ministry (e.g., Acts 22:10; 23:11).

In one case, Agabus, a prophet from Jerusalem, quoted the Holy Spirit, who had given him a supernatural revelation about a future event (Acts 21:10–11). Here, Agabus was speaking the exact words of the Spirit. Agabus was simply a mouthpiece. And the proof of the pudding was in the eating. What Agabus predicted came to pass exactly as the Spirit said it would. It was an authentic prophetic word regarding the future.

However, when we read Paul's letters to the churches, we discover that he never says, "God told me." Rather, he simply speaks what he believes to be God's will in normal, shirtsleeve Greek, using his own vocabulary. And yet, all of what he wrote was inspired by the Spirit of God. The same is true for the other apostles who penned their letters.

What's my point?

It's simply this: I believe that using the "God told me" card is largely a learned habit. It's not the natural way that we Christians speak.

Even if you feel that God has told you something, in most cases, it's profoundly unnecessary to broadcast it to the world so that they know that it was the Almighty, the Creator of the universe who said it to you. Not only that, but I believe it's usually counterproductive and depletes the power of what's being spoken.

To my mind, it's much more natural—and powerful—to simply say what it is that you feel God told you without trying to puff it up by making Him responsible for it.

I've observed that if God has put His words in your mouth or He has given you insight into His thoughts, people will know that it's inspired when you say it. There's no need to "prop it up" by adding the ornament of "God told me" to it.

Of course, if you are an Agabus and you are going to quote the Holy Spirit about something you could only know supernaturally, then by all means go for it. But I will add that many things the Holy Spirit shows us are not meant for us to tell others. They are for our private use. And that use is often to help us know how to effectively minister to others or to know how to intelligently pray for them.

Yet if you feel you must quote the Lord in Agabus-style, I would simply caution you with two things.

One, please use your own natural language. If you're an American, that means speak in shirtsleeve English. No need to dress it up with a dead language from the Elizabethan era *("Thus saith da Laud")*.

Two, if you are quoting God, be aware that *you* are responsible for what you say—not God. At that moment, you are making yourself His mouthpiece.

If it's God, it will be proved to be so.

If it's not, well, it's far better to just say it in your own words without having to add a divine banner to it, making the Lord responsible.

Thus a little revising is in order. Or so it seems to me ...

CHAPTER 3

LET ME PRAY ABOUT IT

REVISING CHRISTIAN CODE LANGUAGE

Did you know that we Christians have a code language? We do. Our code language is pretty common. But it's largely unnoticed.

How many times have you asked a fellow believer for a favor or solicited their help in aiding another person and their response was: "Let me pray about it"? Let me say at the outset that there's absolutely no problem with those five little words—at least, on the surface. And there's no problem with bringing an issue to the Lord and consulting His mind about it. In fact, it's quite commendable.

Yet how many times have you heard these words—"Let me

pray about it"—and then discovered that the person who uttered them never got back to you or they ended up turning down your request?

As I think back on the numerous times I've heard my fellow brothers and sisters in Christ say those words (either to me or to another), the answer invariably ended up being "No." I can think of only a few exceptions.

In short, "Let me pray about it" is Christian code language for "No."

Real-Life Examples

This becomes blatantly obvious when we are presented with some of the most basic issues of life, and we respond by saying, "Let me ask God about it."

Here are some examples of how I've heard this phrase used:

- I used to teach high school. One time a fellow teacher in my department asked one of her peers—a professing Christian—to cover her classroom for one day because she had to tend to her sick child. The Christian responded, "Let me pray about it." She never got back to her fellow teacher. So the teacher had to ask someone else—a non-Christian—to cover her class, and that person did.

- Because her car broke down, a Christian woman needed a ride into work the next morning. The woman asked one of her friends, a believer and a retiree, for the favor. The friend responded, "Let me pray about it, and I'll get back to you." *She never did.*

- A Christian woman wrote to another Christian woman, saying, "I've been starving for Christian fellowship for years. I live in Toledo, Ohio, and I'm desperately looking to find other Christians to gather with. Do you know of any groups of believers in my area that are meeting together?" The reply was: "Yes, there's actually a group in your city that I know and can recommend. Why don't you call them, pay them a visit, and see what you think?" The woman replied, "Let me pray about it." *She never called or visited.*

- A single mother was struggling with a financial need. This was the first time she had such a need; it was not a pattern in her life. So, she reluctantly asked the leadership team of her church for help. Without such help, her electricity would be turned off. The leaders told her, "Give us time to pray about it." They never got back to her, and her electricity was turned off.

- A Christian man hears a report regarding something that several members of a ministry team had allegedly done. Believing the report, he writes a strong email to the team, rebuking and correcting them. The members of the team write back and say that the report he heard was not accurate. The team invites the man to discuss the issue over the phone or in person. The man writes back and says, "Let me pray about it." The members of the team never hear back from him, and the issue goes unresolved.

Observation: Virtually every time I've heard a Christian answer with, "Let me pray about it," there was self-denial involved in the request.

A Glaring Irony

Fellowshipping with Christians over a meal is one of my favorite hobbies. I've had many occasions where I sat in restaurants with other Christians. Not once during those occasions have I ever heard any of them say, "Let me pray about it," when the waitress or waiter came over to the table to take their order.

Yet when it comes to some of the simplest things in life that are presented to us—if some risk or self-denial is involved—many Christians are quick to shroud the ordeal in religious jargon.

Certainly, there are times when we should give a matter over to the Lord and seek His mind on it. I have done this many times in my life and will continue to do so.

But in most situations, I believe knowing the Lord's will is a matter of spiritual instinct and/or of exercising wisdom.[1]

So what's my point?

I'm certainly not suggesting that we give up the practice of bringing things to the Lord's attention and seeking His mind on them, especially those matters that are complex and where our response will affect the lives of others. But "Let me pray about it" has become the universal answer that Christians give to undesired requests.

Forgive the personal illustration, but I think it may help some readers. When I have been faced with a crisis and I need the Lord's precise guidance, I have set myself apart for three days to seek His face on the matter.

In every case, God has been faithful to give me clarity at some point during that three-day period. So I'm not against bringing vital matters before the Lord to discern His mind.

Such cases, however, are the exceptions. As Christians, we *possess* a mind (1 Cor. 2:16; Phil. 2:5 NKJV). We possess a frame of reference where we know by instinct or wisdom what our responses should be in most situations.

What I'm really getting at in this chapter is a plea for honesty.

And an exhortation to not make things "religious" when they don't need to be.

I believe revising ourselves from this sort of Christian code language will take us a long way in reflecting the integrity that's a part of our new identity in Christ.

CHAPTER 4

SPIRITUAL CONVERSATIONAL STYLES

REVISING OUR SEMANTICS

One of the quickest things we pick up as Christians, although quite unconsciously, is a religious vocabulary. Consequently, part of our revising is to identify how we speak and how we hear others speak when discussing spiritual and theological ideas.

The subject of conversational styles is not new. Linguists and sociologists use the term *conversational style* to describe the specific set of assumptions and goals that people employ when they communicate.[1]

All social groups construct such styles to communicate their thoughts. Conversational styles are part of the reason why cross-cultural communication is so difficult. They explain why a French speaker can insist that the meaning of something in French can never be completely rendered in English or German.

It is my observation that many of the misunderstandings and disagreements over spiritual matters arise not out of genuine substantive differences but from differences in communication style.

Oftentimes, a person will use a certain expression to make a theological point (no doubt picked up from his or her denominational background), while his or her discussion partner is made to feel uncomfortable or even offended. The problem of cross talking arises, and the conversation drifts from actual substance to one that gets bogged down in the gears of a diverging style of communication.

Interestingly, the people involved in such discussions are not aware of what's happening. They are only aware of the fact (at least in their own minds) that the conversation has been hijacked because the other person is "hard-hearted," "closed-minded," "biblically ignorant," or "deceived."

If we can get a handle on the different spiritual conversational styles, we will better understand what people actually *believe* rather than focusing on how they *communicate* those beliefs (which can often drive one crazy!). In a nutshell, understanding the reality of spiritual conversational styles (SCSs from henceforth) can move us far ahead in the game of spiritual conversation.

Talking about our SCSs is quite risky. Spiritual beliefs (theology in the broad sense) are very dangerous, for they strike at the heart of what we Christians hold dearest. We construct SCSs to arrange the ground rules upon which spiritual discussions can take place in a way that we find safe and comfortable.

Our SCSs help to insulate our conversations about spiritual things from those ideas that conflict with our own. In this way, SCSs enable us to tread upon the dangerous and terrifying ground of theological debate.

Granted, my discussion of SCSs is subject to abuse. At worst, some may take this chapter and convert it into ammunition by which to stereotype and pigeonhole their fellow brothers and sisters in Christ. At best, it will cause us to look at how we communicate about spiritual matters and encourage us to be better listeners.

I believe the notion of conversational styles is useful because it helps explain why people can routinely misunderstand each other when they appear to share so much in common. It also provides a helpful window into understanding some of the common complexities we face when seeking to cross the line of theological distinctions.

The world of psychotherapy has become such a successful industry in the West because most of us know very little about ourselves—particularly how we think, feel, and react, not to mention how we speak. Understanding SCSs can help us to make progress in how we hear and understand one another.

Keep in mind that identifying a particular SCS in yourself (or in another) is only half the solution to a theological disagreement. The other half is to transcend it and cross-communicate with those who hold to a different SCS than yourself. This is quite difficult, though it's not impossible.

Let me introduce you to what I believe are three of the most common SCSs. As you read through each one, try to populate it with people you have tried to converse with in the past. Hopefully, this chapter will help spare you the agony of talking past other Christians when discussing spiritual matters.

The Charismatic SCS

Those who use the Charismatic SCS tend to be associated with the Charismatic/Pentecostal subculture of the Christian world. In conversation, the Charismatic SCS appeals to personal revelation of the Bible as the authority for interpretation and application.

Advocates of the Charismatic SCS often despise biblical scholarship, paying little attention to the principles of hermeneutics and sound exegesis, deeming them "human" and "man-made." Statements like "the Lord showed me" or "God revealed this to me" or "the Spirit told me" are peppered throughout their conversations.

Those who do not use this particular SCS usually feel quite uncomfortable with such phrases. While they may experience spiritual illumination from the Holy Spirit, they believe it's unbefitting to wield it as a basis of authority.

They also find such claims to divine authority difficult to analyze and inadequate to settle disputes. Not to mention that they believe these declarations often convey the clear impression of "boasting in the flesh." In short, those who do not employ the Charismatic SCS feel that the mere appeal to personal revelation makes the playing field unlevel in the arena of theological discussion.

Here's an example. Suppose that Bill and Chris are discussing a theological issue. Chris uses the Charismatic SCS, while Bill doesn't. After Bill shares an interpretation of a biblical passage with Chris, Chris responds, saying, "The passage does not mean what you say. God showed me that it means thus and so."

In Bill's mind, any attempt at biblical discourse now becomes inadequate, for "God has shown" Chris otherwise. When Bill challenges Chris's position using the principles of exegesis (appealing to historical context, the original meaning of Greek words, etc.), Chris accuses Bill of being "unspiritual," unable to comprehend the language of the Holy Spirit.

Now Bill believes that Chris cannot explain or defend his position academically. He can only appeal to personal revelation.

Therefore, Bill feels that Chris has fallen into the subjective soup of mysticism and is lost in the sauce.

From Bill's vantage point, there's no common ground for communication. The source of authority is neither equal nor mutual. While Chris verbally affirms that Scripture is the measure of all truth and may even push the envelope of biblical authority, in Bill's mind, Chris's appeal to personal revelation demonstrates otherwise. To Chris, Bill is not a spiritual person because he cannot understand or accept the divine inspiration that he (Chris) has received.

In addition, because Bill does not use the mystical jargon that fills Chris's vocabulary, Chris concludes that Bill's relationship with the Holy Spirit is subnormal. Worse still, Chris may judge Bill to not have the Holy Spirit at all, for if he did (he muses to himself), Bill would agree with him.

In effect, Chris is frustrated because he fails to convince Bill of his revelatory encounters (and he may even go so far as to accuse Bill of having a "religious spirit"). Chris doesn't understand why Bill would question his experience, because he is convinced that God speaks to him.

Bill is equally frustrated. He feels that he can't communicate on the same level as Chris. To Bill, Chris's subjective appeals cloud the issue and make the source of authority ambiguous. For Bill, Chris's revelations by no means secure the theological terrain. Chris's discourse, which is cluttered with verbal cues of mystical experiences ("God showed me"), is both unimpressive and unconvincing to Bill.

Chris, on the other hand, is troubled with Bill's "unspirituality" simply because he doesn't share these explicit verbal signals.

So in the end, the person using the Charismatic SCS ends up feeling frustrated and hurt because of his failure to convince those who embrace a different SCS. Likewise, those who disagree with the Charismatic SCS find themselves up against similar frustrations.

There's also a subset of the Charismatic SCS, employed by those who are more familiar with the Bible and the rules of logic. It's marked by the use of a double standard. Such ones invoke both logic and mysticism in their theological communications.

When they attack someone else's interpretation of Scripture, they appeal to the rules of Aristotelian logic. When on the offensive, they say things like, "This interpretation is inconsistent and does not follow. It doesn't mesh well with other scriptural passages." Yet, when they are on the defensive and their conversation partner uses logic to refute their claims, they shift the argument, saying, "I cannot explain this to you ... it transcends logic ... you must have a revelation ... I cannot put the truth into words ... only the Holy Spirit can show this to you," etc.

And the stalemate persists.

The Quoter SCS

People who use the Quoter SCS hinge any meaningful conversation about God to a particular view of biblical authority. The Quoter SCS simply cannot tolerate a spiritual or theological discussion unless the other party shares his or her own assumptions about how the Bible is to be viewed and, more important, how it's to be used.

Most of the folks who use this SCS, particularly in the United States, demand a specific expression of biblical authority. It's the expression that was formulated by American Calvinists in the last century and has been championed by those in modern fundamentalist circles.

The expression is rooted in the belief that the Bible possesses a journalistic type of accuracy concerning events and details. It also affirms that Scripture provides answers to any and every question that's brought to bear on it. To the person who uses the Quoter SCS, such a view of the Bible is a *sine qua non* (a necessary element).

In the eyes of the Quoter SCS, individuals who hold to more moderate views of biblical authority, such as those held by mainstream evangelicals (e.g., Carl F. H. Henry), neoevangelicals (e.g., F. F. Bruce), postconservative evangelicals (e.g., Stanley J. Grenz), and postmodern evangelicals (e.g., N. T. Wright), have departed from sound orthodoxy and are the targets of a prolonged "battle for the Bible" (to use Harold Lindsell's phrase).

The Quoter SCS deems all spiritual discourse to be meaningless without an explicit verbal affirmation by his or her conversation partner that precisely matches his or her own. Without such an affirmation, the Quoter style's level of comfort in discussing spiritual things becomes violated and proves inadequate to carry on a theological discussion. At best, Quoters simply lose interest in the topic. At worst, they benightedly conclude that their discussion partner is a heretic!

For the Quoter SCS, the only way to settle a theological dispute is by quoting Scripture. The mere act of Bible-quoting is thought to set defensible boundaries for theological discussions to take place.

There's no problem with quoting the Bible. The biblical authors themselves quoted Scripture in abundant measure. However, the Quoter SCS believes that theological disputes are settled by the *simple* quoting of Scripture and nothing more. Historical context is typically ignored. Instead, the art of "proof-texting" is employed to settle all disagreements.

(Another version of the Quoter is the person who appeals to the authority of a favorite theologian. Such naked assertions as "Calvin said," "Luther said," "Augustine said" to settle arguments are punctuated throughout their discussions.)

Let me illustrate how the Quoter SCS operates. Suppose that Steve uses the Quoter SCS, while Jack does not. Whenever Steve disagrees with Jack, he quotes a raft of Scriptures. Yet in his quoting, Steve gives no attention to context, historical setting, or the original meaning of Greek or Hebrew words. Rather, Steve appeals solely to a bundle of isolated texts that he believes buttress his position.

In the aftermath of his endless quoting, Steve retorts with something like "See, the Bible is clear about this. Here are the verses. Believe it or reject it!" (Granted, not everyone who uses this style is as curt as I've painted Steve, but you get the idea.)

By his quoting, Steve has implicitly and explicitly conveyed a sense of finality to the issue. But to Jack, Steve's quoting hasn't settled anything at all. In fact, Jack is outraged by the mere notion that it has. Steve, on the other hand, concludes that Jack doesn't want to listen to the Bible and ends the discussion there.

Jack finds Steve's stylistic conventions to be shallow and unconvincing at best. He regards them to be strident, combative, and demeaning at worst. Jack's complaint is that Steve is utilizing naive hermeneutics, isolated proof-texting, and is ignoring the "whole" of Scripture. To Jack, the aggressive penchant to simply quote the Bible as if that in itself settles the questions of the universe is silly. In addition, Jack feels that Steve is essentially hiding behind his quotes, fearing rigorous dialogue that may shatter his rigid theological framework.

In short, the Quoter SCS feels safe and secure under the arsenal of isolated proof texts that he's managed to string together to defend his position. Any dialogue about what those texts actually mean by appealing to their historical setting and original rendering is shrugged off as irrelevant.

To the practitioners of the Quoter SCS, nothing can be argued after the simple and direct appeal to a biblical reference has been made, even if that reference is isolated from the rest of the Bible. Too often, the Quoter SCS finds himself caught in a parenthesis of disagreement, when the root problem beyond the controversy is subtly masquerading beneath the pious rhetoric of "faithfully defending the Word."

The Pragmatic SCS

Unlike the Charismatic SCS and the Quoter SCS, the Pragmatic SCS is chiefly interested in what works. Those who use this style have a nuts-and-bolts approach to life. Appeals to personal revelation do not impress them. Neither do quotes from the Bible. They want to see what is working and what has proved to be successful in the lives of the people with whom they converse. This, they believe, is where truth lies.

Those who hold to the Pragmatic SCS believe that there are no easy answers to the countless theological questions that have raged in the church for the last seventeen centuries. Rather than quibbling about "correct doctrine," the Pragmatic SCS focuses his or her sights on what is working in the real world. With this in mind, the Pragmatic SCS is concerned less with academic differences and centers more on actual practice. Pragmatics are also willing to "agree to disagree" over theological matters.

Of course, this approach does not sit well with those who are less charitable and more militant in spirit, insisting upon resolving their differences "for the sake of the truth." While this sounds noble, it often tends toward division and harsh feelings. Nevertheless, the Pragmatic SCS is always pressing the question "How has this truth worked in *your* life, in *your* church, etc.?"

Those who do not use the Pragmatic SCS feel uncomfortable with this approach. They believe that such a rearrangement of the conversational furniture betrays the authority of Scripture. Since the Pragmatic style is more concerned with outward effects, it pays less attention to doctrinal precision. Hence, when a Quoter cites a text from Matthew, the Pragmatic isn't satisfied. He or she wants to know "How does this work out in real life?" Their conviction is that evaluating the practical outworking of a given belief is much richer than merely quoting a biblical text and less likely to short out the conversation.

Those who use different stylistic conventions argue that the Pragmatic approach rests upon shaky ground as a basis for one's beliefs. They feel that just because a belief may appear to have practical utility, that doesn't mean it's valid or divinely approved. Thus when Quoters and Pragmatics have conversations, both seek to cajole each other into rearranging the boundaries of the conversation so that the other person is conversing according to their playbook. This is largely true with the Charismatic style as well, for if God hasn't spoken something directly to his or her conversational partner, the Charismatic is apt to reject it, regardless of its practical utility or biblical merit.

It must be stressed at this point that not all who hold to the Pragmatic SCS work with the same premise. For some Pragmatics, the notion of success is a self-evident idea that's measured by outward metrics like numbers, size, budget, attendance, conversions, etc. For others, the concept of success lies in following Christ and being conformed to His image. However, because of the strong appeal to success and workability, these two versions of the Pragmatic SCS are often indistinguishable by other SCSs.

Conclusion

Ironically, all three spiritual conversational styles honestly affirm biblical authority. But each is too unwilling to hear this affirmation in terms other than its own. For this reason, misunderstandings abound when Christians discuss spiritual and theological matters.

When going into such discussions, advocates of each style are often overconfident that they'll persuade the other with their own viewpoint. But not long after, they discover that they have found themselves dashed headlong into an unbridled, frustrated tension that frequently leads to virtual insanity on the one hand or division on the other.

Understanding SCSs can help us to have more profitable discussions with our fellow sisters and brothers in Christ. The challenge is to swallow our initial reactions to someone else's SCS and seek to grasp what is behind their less-than-perfect speech style. In this way, Charismatics, Quoters, and Pragmatics alike will no longer shanghai each other into pointless and unprofitable discussions. Instead, they will learn to listen to what each is seeking to communicate.[2]

In addition, each of the three SCSs would do well to learn from the other two. For example, the Quoter should learn the importance of the practical things of life. The Pragmatic should take the Bible more seriously, etc.

Understanding an SCS, either your own or that of another, is not a cure-all for resolving a disagreement over a spiritual matter. Not every theological battle finds its roots in a conflicting SCS. Yet, if we are revising ourselves to better understand the way in which we communicate, we'll be brought further along in our attempt to learn Jesus Christ from one another.

CHAPTER 5

WHAT'S WRONG WITH OUR GOSPEL?

REVISING OUR MESSAGE

Paul of Tarsus used the phrase "my gospel" numerous times in his letters. He was referring to the message that he preached.

While there's nothing wrong with *Paul's* gospel, I do have concerns about what's missing from *our* gospel—that is, the gospel that many Christians are hearing today.

I've written an entire book on this subject.[1] But in this chapter, I'd like to focus on five elements that seem to be missing from our gospel that were a large part of the gospel presented by Jesus and the apostles.

Of course, your mileage may vary. And if it does, that's great. But a large portion of the Christian world today has neglected a number of vital elements of the gospel. Here are five of them:

1. The Reality of an Indwelling Lord

There's a great deal of emphasis today on being like Christ. This is commonly tied into and even defined as "discipleship." The way to be like Christ, it is taught, is by imitating His behavior.

I believe that this emphasis is correct. But it's not complete.

Christian leaders have been telling God's people that they must "be like Christ" for the last six hundred years (at least). The well-known book by Thomas à Kempis, *The Imitation of Christ*, was published around 1418.

Some 480 years later, Charles M. Sheldon's book *In His Steps: What Would Jesus Do?* was published. Ever since then, Christians have been trying to "do what Jesus did."

But this "gospel" hasn't worked. The reason? It's an instance of asking the wrong question. The question is not "What would Jesus do?" I believe it's "What *is* Jesus Christ *doing* through me … and through us?"

Jesus made pretty clear that *we* cannot live the Christian life. Instead, He must live it through us.

> *I am the vine; you are the branches. If a man remains*
> *in me and I in him, he will bear much fruit; apart*
> *from me you can do nothing. (John 15:5)*

Notice that Jesus Himself couldn't live the Christian life without His Father:[2]

> *Jesus gave them this answer: "I tell you the truth, the*
> *Son can do nothing by himself; he can do only what*
> *he sees his Father doing." (John 5:19)*

> *By myself I can do nothing; I judge only as I hear,*
> *and my judgment is just, for I seek not to please*
> *myself but him who sent me. (John 5:30)*

Unlike all other religions, the founder of our faith is still alive. But that's not all.

He lives inside of all who have repented and believed upon Him.

But that's not all.

As Christians, we have been called to *live by* His indwelling life. And we can.

Note Jesus' own words:

As the living Father hath sent me, and I live by the
Father: so he that eateth me, even he shall live by
me. (John 6:57 KJV)

A large part of the gospel is to be awakened to an indwelling Christ—not as a doctrine or theology, but as a living, breathing Person whose life we can live by.

Paul's central message was "Not I, but Christ" and "Christ in you, the hope of glory." (See Rom. 8; Col. 1; Gal. 2; and John 14—17, where Jesus Himself spoke about His indwelling just before His death.) Paul said, "To live is Christ," which means that Jesus, being in the Spirit, can now serve with our hands, walk with our feet, see with our eyes, and speak with our lips.

Jesus Christ lived His life by an indwelling Father. In the same way, we as believers can live the Christian life only by an indwelling Christ.

This is not a peripheral issue; it's a central part of the gospel.

Imitating Jesus, therefore, is not a matter of trying to mimic the outward things He did (as if we can actually do that in our own energy).

It's rather a matter of imitating the *way* He lived His life. It's to get in touch with the engine of His outward activities and to "do likewise."

This puts us on a collision course with the issue of living by an indwelling Lord.

In short, the goal of the gospel is not to get you out of hell and into heaven, but to get God out of heaven and into you so that He may be displayed visibly and glorified in His creation.

2. The Greatness of Christ

Some Christian groups present the Christ of Romans and Galatians. He's come to save the lost.

Others present the Christ of the Gospels. His earthly life must be imitated.

Some groups present the Christ of the cross. His death is emphasized above everything else.

Others groups present the Christ of Easter. His resurrection is primary.

All of the above emphasize the Christ of earthly history.

But there is the Christ who exists before time.

And there is the Christ of the present and the future.

And all are the same Christ.

Creation was created *in* the Son of God before time and when He was made the First Born of all creation (Col. 1). Further, God the Father chose all of His people *in* Christ before time (Eph. 1).

After His resurrection, the Lord Jesus Christ sat at the right hand of God as Lord of heaven and earth. Today, He intercedes for us, acts as our High Priest, loves us as our Shepherd, and lives out His indwelling life in and through us.

As the Alpha and Omega, time is within Christ. Jesus knows no beginning and no end. All of creation is moving toward Christ being Head over all, in all, through all, and to all, "that He might fill all things" (Eph. 4:10 NASB).

In the end, all things will be summed up in this incredible Christ (Eph. 1:10; 4:10).

And this is the Christ who has taken up residence within you and me (Gal. 2:20; Rom. 8:10; Col. 1:27).

3. The Eternal Purpose of God

With few exceptions, *our* gospel begins with Genesis 3 rather than Genesis 1. Our starting point is the fall of humanity.

The result: Everything is framed around God's redemptive mission. It's all about saving a lost world.

Part of the reason for this, I believe, is that evangelical Christians have built their theology mostly on Romans and Galatians. And many nonevangelical Christians have built it on the Gospels (particularly the Synoptics—Matthew, Mark, and Luke). And for both groups, Ephesians and Colossians have been put in the footnotes.

But what if we began not with the needs of humans but with the intent and purpose of God? What if we took as our point of departure not the earth after the fall but the eternal activity within God Himself before the constraints of physical time?

In other words, what if we built our theology on Ephesians

and Colossians and allowed the other New Testament books to follow suit?

Why Ephesians and Colossians? Because these two letters give us the clearest look at Paul's gospel with which Christ commissioned him. These two letters begin not with the needs of postfall humans but with God's timeless purpose before creation. They also introduce us to Christ in His preincarnate state.

I assert that if we did this, the Gospels and the rest of the New Testament (let alone the entire Old Testament) would fall into a very different place for us.

The Gospels are not the beginning point of the Christian faith. Neither is the Old Testament. Both give us the middle of the story. Ephesians, Colossians, and the gospel of John are the introduction and the opening chapters of that story. Those writings give us a glimpse into Christ before time and what His original intention is all about.

In this regard, we can liken the gospel that many of us have heard to watching *Star Wars* Episodes IV, V, and VI first (which is the way they came out in the theaters).

But for us to really understand what's going on in that drama, we must begin at the right place with Episodes I, II, and III.

Consider this fact. Human beings didn't come into this world in need of salvation. There was a purpose in God that came before the fall, and He has never let go of it.[3]

Without an understanding of God's ageless purpose, our good deeds can be likened to playing an instrument on our own as opposed to playing with others as part of an orchestra that is performing one breathtaking song.

4. It Takes God to Be Human

We all were born into Adam. We were all born into an old, fallen, corrupt humanity. Strikingly, God has chosen not to renovate, improve, or correct the old humanity. Instead, He has chosen to do one thing with it.

Crucify it.

We got into Adam by birth. The only way to get out of him and his race is by death. And the only way to get into Christ is by birth. New birth.

Note Paul's words: "Knowing this, that our old man has been crucified with Him" (Rom. 6:6 NKJV), and "I have been crucified with Christ and I no longer live, but *Christ lives in me*" (Gal. 2:20).

You aren't really human until you've died and risen again. The good news is that this has already happened (Rom. 6—8).

The old Adam cannot be cosmetically adjusted, repaired, or improved.

He must be put to death.

Jesus Christ was a living portrait of God's thought for humanity. He was the true human.

In His resurrection, Jesus became the Head of a new humanity that transcends the old distinctions of race and gender (Gal. 3:28; Col. 3:10–11; 2 Cor. 5:17). The Man, Jesus, is what God intended humanity to be. He was a Person who lived by God's life. In the same way, every person today who lives by the life of God is revealing their true humanity.

So it takes God to be human.

Adam and Eve were offered the Tree of Life in the garden. But they never partook of it. God's intention from the beginning was for humans to live by divine life.

And here's the good news: Jesus Christ is the reality of the Tree of Life. He has been offered to us today to partake of (John 6:57). We can partake of Him now and thus be fully human and part of a new humanity—a new creation—a new kind of human.

What a beautiful way to present the gospel to those who don't know Jesus: Here is a way to become fully human. Receive Jesus Christ, the Head of the new humanity.

No other religion offers such a glorious prospect.

5. Everything Wears Out Except for Christ

Albert Einstein once said that the definition of insanity is doing the same thing over and over again and expecting different results.

I often feel that way about contemporary Christianity. As an observer of the passing parade, I've noted the following: Most of what's put on the table with respect to reforming and renewing the church are the same ideas repackaged from decade to decade.

There's very little *new* in any of them.

But more critical, these "renewing" and "reforming" ideas and solutions lack one critical element. That element is best illustrated by what Steve Jobs, the CEO of Apple, once said during an interview:

> *Lots of companies have tons of great engineers and smart people. But ultimately, there needs to be some gravitational force that pulls it all together. Otherwise, you can get great pieces of technology all floating around the universe. But it doesn't add up to much.... There were bits and pieces of interesting things floating around, but not that gravitational pull.*[4]

Jobs's metaphor is an apt description of the great need in the church today. Christians have made the gospel about so many "interesting things floating around" but without *the* gravitational pull that brings them all together.

And that gravitational pull is the Lord Jesus Christ.

That said, if there's anything I've learned by being a Christian over the last thirty years, it's this:

- Any solution, cure, or remedy that doesn't have Jesus Christ at its center is doomed to fail.

- Everything in the Christian life eventually wears out. The only thing that doesn't is Christ Himself. He is new every morning.[5]

Consequently, all of our methods, techniques, innovative ideas, strategies, programs, and solutions don't stand a chance if the Lord Jesus Himself isn't front and center of them all.

He and He alone is God's method, technique, idea, strategy, program, and solution.

He is the way, the truth, and the life (John 14:6).

Christ and Christ alone is the gospel (2 Cor. 4:5). Everything else tastes like plain yogurt.

CHAPTER 6

THE FELT-PRESENCE OF GOD

REVISING OUR AWARENESS OF THE DIVINE

In 1993, what came to be known as the "Toronto Blessing" hit the United States. Rodney Howard-Browne held his first convention in the Carpenter's Home Church in Lakeland, Florida.

That convention went on for weeks. From there, it quickly spread to other parts of North America—most notably Toronto, Canada; Melbourne, Florida; and Pensacola, Florida.

Upon hearing about the new move of God in March 1993, I traveled to Lakeland and sat in on those first meetings where "the blessing" had just begun. In January 1996, I traveled to Melbourne,

Florida, and attended a meeting officiated by Randy Clark when the phenomenon had spread there in full force.

I won't get into too much detail about my time in these meetings, but I'm glad I attended them.

Ever since I've been a Christian, I've had an insatiable hunger to know my Lord more deeply. If I hear a report that God is uniquely at work in a given place, I'll move heaven and earth to visit it. This is what prompted me to check out those early meetings in Lakeland and Melbourne.

One thing I saw in those meetings is something I have observed ever since I've been a Christian. Namely, a large portion of the Christian population is seeking a fresh touch from God. *They are seeking to experience His presence.*

Some, however, appear to be almost pathologically dependent upon trying to "feel" God's presence. For these souls, "feeling" the presence of the Lord becomes a benchmark to measure their spiritual condition.

I spent most of my early Christian life drinking deeply from the wells of a particular movement that stressed the miraculous power of God. While I learned many valuable lessons in that movement, I also have a few reservations. One of them is that the propensity to seek "the felt-presence of God" in that movement is central and overwhelming.

I watched many Christians struggle with this quest to the

point of concluding that something was wrong with them—that God loved them less—all because they weren't "feeling" or "sensing" His presence on a regular basis.

On the other hand, I have known Christian women and men who were utterly devoted to the Lord, extremely gifted, spiritually insightful and fruitful. Yet in private, their confession was that they had *never* "felt" the presence of God.

I've also personally known Christians who were in dire spiritual straits. Some were living double lives. Yet they didn't wince at their poor condition, because during worship services or prayer times they regularly "felt" the presence of God.

This being said, I believe there's a great deal of confusion over the matter of God's presence. Part of it is rooted in semantics. Another part is rooted in bad theology. Either way, it's an area where revision is desperately needed.

Let's look at the semantic problem first. (Semantics refers to the words we use to express certain concepts.)

The Semantics of God's Presence

Some Christians have a way of overstating their experiences. Others understate them. Multiple people may experience the exact same phenomenon—whether it be a church meeting, a conference, a retreat, a convention, a particular manifestation of the Holy Spirit, or a shared encounter.

One person may describe it as "unbelievable!" ... "incredible!" ... "awesome!" ... "beyond description!" Another may describe it as "refreshing" ... "enjoyable" ... "encouraging" ... "delightful." Still another may describe it as "good" ... "fine" ... "a blessing."

Point: People often use very different vocabulary to express the exact same thing. For instance, Watchman Nee used a unique phrase when he referred to his fellowship with the Lord. He called it "touching the Lord." Others use the phrase "sweet communion." Others use "divine encounter." Others use less phenomenological phrases.

To describe fixing one's heart upon the Lord, some people use the phrase "turning to the Lord." Others use the word "gazing." Others say "beholding" or "looking into the face of God." Still others say "contemplating," "centering," "abiding," or "partaking." Others describe it as "meditating."

By and large, it's semantics.

I've observed this phenomenon all my Christian life. People express the same experiences differently. This is due to many varied factors, some of which are the person's temperament, the specific vocabulary of one's religious tradition, or a specific "effect" they wish to have on those who hear them testify. (Sometimes this isn't so well motivated.)

In addition, to say that a Christian is to "seek" a feeling of

God's presence is bad theology. There's no such exhortation in all of Scripture. Try to find it in the New Testament, and you will discover that it's glaringly absent. It's just not there.

An oft-quoted passage used to support the idea of seeking God's felt-presence is Psalm 22:3. In the King James Version, it reads, "Thou [God] that inhabitest the praises of Israel." This text has been traditionally used to invoke or summon God's presence by singing praise and worship songs.

Strikingly, except for the King James Version, the New Jerusalem Bible, and the New Century Version, most other versions translate it differently. For instance, the Revised English Bible translates it this way: "You, the praise of Israel, are enthroned in the sanctuary."

The New American Bible takes the same approach: "Yet you are enthroned as the Holy One; you are the glory of Israel." The New International Version does likewise: "Yet you are enthroned as the Holy One; you are the praise of Israel." The New Living Translation translates it as follows: "Yet you are holy, enthroned on the praises of Israel."

The term *praise* here is seen as a reference to the One whom Israel praises. The text is an affirmation of an Old Testament reality. Simply put, the presence of God dwells in the Holy of Holies in the temple at Jerusalem. It in no way indicates that God is somehow made present by our praises.

According to the scholars who have translated this passage in the above versions, (1) the text must be understood in the context of Old Testament temple worship, and (2) it is God Himself in His presence in the temple who is called "the Praise (or Glory) of Israel."

What's more, we must be cautious about literally applying statements about Old Testament temple worship to Christian worship. Consider the implications of Jesus' words in John 4 in this regard.

> *Believe me, woman, a time is coming when you will worship the Father neither on this mountain nor in Jerusalem.... Yet a time is coming and has now come when the true worshipers will worship the Father in spirit and truth, for they are the kind of worshipers the Father seeks. God is spirit, and his worshipers must worship in spirit and in truth. (John 4:21, 23–24)*

Worship of the living God can occur at any place and at any time.

Distinctions of God's Presence

Let's draw some distinctions about God's presence. These are my own linguistic handles and definitions:

- *The Reality of God's Presence*—when God is *actually* present in or with a person or group of people.

- *The Felt-Presence of God*—the *perceptible* and *evident* sense or feeling of God's presence.

- *The Deliberate Consciousness of God's Presence*—when one's mind and heart are actively set upon the Lord.

- *The Background Consciousness of God's Presence*—the *unnoticed* but *ever-present* consciousness of God's presence. (More on this later.)

Here are some candid observations on the presence of God— revisions that I hope will bring clarity to the issue:

(1) God Is Always Present with His People

God is *always* present in the life of a believer—whether one actively feels His presence or not. Jesus Christ Himself promised His followers, "I will never leave you nor forsake you" (Heb. 13:5 NKJV).

To put it another way, the *reality* of God's presence is always with the Christian, and it doesn't change. It's not dependent on or evidenced by feelings or senses.

The New Testament is quite loud in its proclamation that God in Christ dwells in every believer by the Holy Spirit (Rom. 8:1–17). This is an unmovable fact. To state it personally, you, dear Christian, are *always* in God's presence! His presence is not something you need to seek. It's not something you need to acquire. The presence of God is not something to be invoked, summoned, or sought after. It's an ever-present reality for all Christians.

As Paul said to the Romans, you don't need to go to heaven to bring Christ down. Nor do you need to go to the depths to bring Christ up. *He is in you ... nearer than your breath is to your mouth.* You have access to Him at every moment (Rom. 10:6–13).

(2) Believing That God Is

There is a great difference between the "felt-presence" of God and the "deliberate consciousness" of His presence. To be conscious of His presence is to be "intentionally aware" that He is with you and in you.

Hebrews 11:6 (KJV) says, "But without faith it is impossible to please him: for he that cometh to God must believe that he is, and that he is a rewarder of them that diligently seek him."

Psalm 46:10 (KJV) echoes the thought, saying, "Be still, and know that I am God."

How do you become deliberately conscious of God's presence? By simply placing your attention upon Him. To "be still and know" that "God is" is to be intentionally conscious of His presence.

In Paul's words, to be conscious of God's presence is to "set your mind on the Spirit" (see Rom. 8:5–6). Some Christians call the deliberate consciousness of God's presence "being *in* His presence." Technically, that's not correct. We are *always* in His presence, because He lives in us. Practically, however, to be "in His presence" is simply to turn your attention upon the Lord. To turn to Him with loving attentiveness.

One can be intentionally conscious of God's presence by a simple act of faith. Let me give an illustration. Your nose is always with you, correct? It's a part of you. However, you can go all day long and never once give attention to your nose. Does this mean that you are no longer in the presence of your nose? No. It simply means that you can be unconscious of it.

In the same way, the Lord is always with you. But you can go about your busy day and never once acknowledge or think about Him. You can set your mind on earthly things and never once be conscious of the Lord who indwells you. On the contrary, by setting your mind and heart upon Him, you become actively conscious of His presence (Rom. 8:5–7; Col. 3:1–4).

(3) The Secret to Spiritual Formation

The secret to spiritual formation is to be conscious of God's presence as much as possible. Why? Imagine that Jesus Christ physically appeared to you right now. And He went with you wherever you went. You physically saw Him at all times. He was visibly with you every waking moment. Would this have any effect on your conduct and behavior? The answer is obviously *yes*.

The twelve disciples were changed simply by being *with* Him. "And they [the leaders of the Sanhedrin] took note that these men [Peter and John] had *been with* Jesus" (Acts 4:13). Brother Lawrence called the deliberate consciousness of God's presence the art of "practicing His presence." For Brother Lawrence, to practice God's presence was to be mindful of Him all day long. It also included conversing with Him throughout the day.

This would be akin to drawing my attention to my nose constantly. Although my nose is always with me, I may or may not be conscious of it. It all depends on where my attention is centered.

(4) The Feeling of God's Presence

It is possible to have experiences where one is overwhelmed with the "feeling" or "sense" of God's nearness, His majesty, His power, His love, His favor, or His union and oneness with the believer. To put it another way, it's possible to have a "sense" or "feeling" of His presence.

However, I am of the strong opinion that we should not "seek" such feelings. Nor should we make the profound mistake of regarding such feelings as a gauge or measure of spirituality or spiritual formation.

Permit me to speak personally for a moment. In my own life, I have had numerous occasions where I felt overwhelmed with God's love, grace, and nearness to the point of weeping profusely. (I used to be embarrassed by this, but I've learned to just accept it. It's how I typically react when I'm overwhelmed by the Lord's majesty, power, and love.)

I've had times when I felt God's power so strong that I *physically* couldn't contain it. I literally felt like I was going to explode. I've also known times when I "smelled" the fragrance of His presence and other times when I had ecstatic experiences too deep for words. (I cannot explain any of these experiences rationally by the way.)

However, *none* of these experiences were a measure of my spiritual condition. Nor did they indicate God's sentiments toward me at a particular time, as though His feelings for me changed with the wind or were based on my conduct. Further, I have learned not to *seek* such experiences. If they come, they come. If I never have them again, it doesn't change the fact that I'm *always* in His presence and that He is *always* with me.

God's love and favor toward me remain unchanged. They

cannot be altered, for they are based not on my work, but upon the work of Another—Jesus Christ. In addition, I've learned to delight in the quiet rest that comes from just turning my attention upon Him—whether that be in a time of silent stillness before Him or throughout the day when I'm in constant fellowship with Him.

This discovery is not novel. It is echoed by many of the spiritual writers of the past. A number of them have stated rather strongly that to seek "spiritual" delights is just as harmful as seeking "worldly" ones. And it's possible to fall in love with the sense of God's presence but fail to love God Himself.

(5) When God Walks Off the Stage

A Christian in the sixteenth century coined the term *the dark night of the soul*. This phrase refers to an experience when God removes the "sense" of His presence from a believer's life. Some Christians believe that the "dark night" is an exotically rare experience that few people have. Others believe it's much more common. I tend to be in the camp that believes it's rare.

The dark night is when God tosses out the moral compass from a believer's life. The Christian feels as though God doesn't exist. This is neither a dry spell nor a punishment. Instead, it feels as though God has left. The inner consciousness of the Lord's presence is swept away without warning, and only a blind reliance on past faith saves the Christian from becoming an atheist. This is not the consequence of sin or rebellion. In fact, it has nothing to do with a believer's conduct at all.

Here are the words of a person who is experiencing the dark night: "I feel like a non-Christian. He's just not there anymore. I never noticed His presence until it left me. Now I long for it again. I feel like the ground under me has been ripped away. My joy is gone. I feel out of control. My spiritual feelings are dull. I've lost interest in and affection for God. When I try to speak to Him, it feels like I'm talking to myself or to the ceiling. Prayer once came easy; I talked to the Lord all the time. Now it's forced. It feels like there's a big wall between me and God. My love for the Lord has been replaced by a blank. I never knew what God's presence felt like until it was removed from me. I cry a lot now. I want Him to return to me again."

Some have called the dark night "a game of love" where God plays hide-and-seek. Others view it as a sign of spiritual maturity and development where God is removing the training wheels. In such cases, the Lord is teaching His children how to know Him apart from feelings. He's seeking to show them a new way of relating to Him—one that is more mature and doesn't rely on anything but faith.

If, perchance, you're going through this mysterious experience right now, the one piece of advice I can give you is this: Keep in mind that the dark night is simply a crisis and pathway to greater spiritual maturity. God is still with you. In fact, He's behind this experience. The overarching purpose is redemptive and constructive. I will not expound on the dark night beyond the above except to illustrate one point. Let's return to our nose analogy. During the course of the day, you are virtually unconscious of the presence of your nose. The exception is when you have a sniffle, a nose itch, a nosebleed, or when you look in the mirror. But if you were to have surgery and your nose was removed, you would certainly be conscious that something essential was missing. And that consciousness would remain for quite a long time.

As I said in the opening of this chapter, there is something called "the background consciousness of God's presence." If God were to remove this background consciousness, you would know it immediately. The background consciousness of God's presence is largely undetected and unnoticed by us Christians. We don't recognize it for one simple reason: *It's always present.* It's not dissimilar to why you don't notice the ring on your finger or the watch on your wrist at every moment. You don't notice it because it's *always* there.

However, if the consciousness of God's ever-abiding presence were removed, it would register heavily upon you. (This is what happens when someone experiences the dark night of the soul.)

So in one regard, we are always conscious of the divine presence in that we are *used* to it. The light of God is *always* on. But it looms in the background. Yet at another level, we can be *deliberately* conscious of His presence. We can be focused on His presence in the foreground. We can be attentive to it.

At this point you might ask: *How do I begin to become deliberately conscious of God's presence?* There are many ways, but they are beyond the scope of this book. For the purposes of this chapter, however, I will introduce you to one of the simplest ways that will also help make my overriding point.

At this very moment, turn your attention on the Lord who is always with you and who is always in you. Open your mouth and say to Him, "Lord Jesus, I need You."

As soon as you do, you are *consciously practicing* His presence or whatever other name you wish to assign to it. This is true regardless of what your senses or feelings may say.

God's presence is deeper than any human sensation or perception.

Continue this simple practice the rest of your life, and you will have found one of the wellsprings and mainstays of spiritual formation.

CHAPTER 7

CAPTURED BY THE SAME SPIRIT YOU OPPOSE

REVISING OUR ATTITUDES

Numerous things about the Christian life amaze me. One of them has to do with a phenomenon that has repeated itself throughout church history. I call it "being captured by the same spirit you oppose."

I was first introduced to this phenomenon while reading the work of a well-known sixteenth-century Reformer. He was writing about the infinite evils of inflicting violence upon his fellow Christian brethren over doctrinal disputes. This man was the leader of one of the best-known denominations during the Reformation.

At the time, his group was being mercilessly persecuted by the accepted church of his day.

As I was reading his impassioned indictment against persecuting fellow members of the body of Christ, my jaw dropped in bewilderment. The reason? This same man and his movement were responsible for slaughtering countless numbers of Anabaptist Christians in the most cruel and gruesome ways over doctrinal differences!

What happened to this man?

He had been captured by the same spirit that he opposed. And as typically is the case, he was blissfully unaware of it.

For me, this was more than a history lesson. I've watched this same phenomenon happen so many times that I've lost count.

For Instance

Recently, I was talking to a friend who spent considerable time with a certain minister. My friend told me that this minister condemned the evils of sectarianism, elitism, and arrogance more clearly, more eloquently, and more articulately than any person he had ever met in his life. This minister also spoke vehemently against being dishonest and using unethical methods in the Lord's work.

Shockingly, my friend went on to explain how this same minister happened to be one of the most sectarian, elitist, and arrogant individuals he had ever met in his entire life. And the minister was also incredibly dishonest and unethical. He built the kingdom with one hand while tearing it down with the other.

How could this be?

He had been captured by the same spirit he opposed.

History is rife with examples of this. In the early nineteenth century, two movements that were born of God emerged on the Christian horizon. Both originated in Ireland. One spread to the United States; the other spread to England. Both began around 1830.

The founding fathers of both movements sought to restore the primitive expression of the early church. Both abhorred divisions in the body of Christ. And both sought to recapture the unity of the Christian family.

Yet as time went on, the members of each movement began to gripe with one another over doctrinal matters. The disputing became so intense that both movements split into multiple sects, all of which fought bitterly with one another. Each faction believed that the truth lived and died with them.

Both movements crystallized into denominations that came to regard all other Christians as standing outside the pale of authentic Christian truth. They began to view all other believers as being unwittingly deceived at best or heretical at worst.

Ironically, both movements were founded by men who resolved to end sectarianism and establish unity among all Christians. Yet both ended up spawning some of the most sectarian and elitist groups in Christian history. Each one turned out to be a case of high ideals gone dysfunctional.

What happened? Both movements were captured by the same spirit they set out to oppose.

"Diversity without division, unity without uniformity" is a beautiful slogan. But those who are captured by the same spirit they oppose always end up betraying it in practice.

The Root Cause

Now why does this happen? What's the source of being captured by the same spirit one opposes?

I have my ideas and speculations, but I don't pretend to know the answer. In fact, the purpose of this chapter is not to try and offer an answer. Instead, it's to make the point loud and clear that we are *all* susceptible to this spirit. Like any sin or shortcoming, none of us is immune. Each of us needs a steady dose of God's infinite grace to avoid falling sway to it.

I will simply say that anytime God moves through an individual or group, this spirit crouches at the door, waiting to jump out of the bushes and capture its prey.

Since God is once again blowing on His church today in some fresh ways, it's imperative that we understand the danger of being captured by the same spirit we oppose.

What follows are some specific observations I've made over the years regarding how this spirit works. I trust that isolating them here will help us all to avoid being captured by it.

(1) Judging Motives

Those who are captured by the same spirit they oppose tend to impute the motives of their own hearts onto those who threaten them. Christian leaders who have inflated egos or deep insecurities are easily threatened by others. As a result, they will unwittingly read their own heart motives into the hearts of other people.

Psychologists call this "projection." I can't face my own shortcomings and defects so I unconsciously project them onto other people. I accuse others of the very same dark things that are lurking deep within my own heart.

I've watched some Christian leaders engage in projection when they came into contact with those who were just as (or more) gifted than they were. The root was jealousy. You can call it a "Saul complex," if you will.

Herein lies a great lesson: *Those who judge the motives of others are simply revealing what's in their own hearts.*

In Matthew 7:1–4, Jesus points out that those with defective eyesight are all too willing to perform eye surgery on others. Yet within this text, the Lord makes this chilling assessment:

If you impute an evil motive onto someone else, you're simply making known what *your* motives are.

To put it another way, the piece of sawdust we see in our brother's eye is simply a small chip off the two-by-four that lies within our own. And a piece of wood will always distort our vision.

When people cannot face the reality of what's in their own hearts, they project it onto others—particularly those who they find threatening to their egos.

One of the most profound influences in my life was a talk radio show host from many years back. When this man first broke into the talk radio business, he sat at the feet of a man whom he idolized. He was this talk radio show host's mentor. We'll call the mentor "Nelson" since I don't wish to disclose his name.

When Nelson discovered that the man who he had mentored began to surpass him in popularity, all hell broke loose. Nelson's monstrous ego began to flicker, and he was loaded for bear. He launched the first salvo, and the two men waged an on-the-air radio slap fight that marched off the map of dignity.

Pointed insults were swapped. Disparaging remarks were cast. Both men drew blood from one another, and the listeners got caught up in the carnage. It turned out to devolve into something quite vicious, and the exchange deeply hurt my radio friend.

Unfortunately, no one could reel in the egos or squash the infighting. It turned into bad blood. Nelson was radioactive for quite some time, and the two men didn't speak a civil word to each other for many years.

What happened to these two men is not an isolated incident. I've watched it occur numerous times since I've been a Christian. King Saul is not the only gifted man who has been threatened by a younger David.

What was at the root of that painful period in David's life? Jealousy and envy in the heart of Saul and the threatening feeling (as well as the irrational paranoia) that comes with them.

> As they danced, they sang: "Saul has slain his thousands, and David his tens of thousands." Saul was very angry; this refrain galled him. "They have credited David with tens of thousands," he thought, "but me with only thousands. What more can he get but the kingdom?" (1 Sam. 18:7–8)

Incidentally, jealousy and envy are what provoked the religious leaders of our Lord's day to put Him to death. Tragically, this same drama has played out since Cain slew his younger brother out of jealousy.

I'm no fan of Sigmund Freud nor of his theory of the Oedipus complex. (Please reread that last sentence.) But what led Freud to construct his oedipal theory was a legitimate observation about human nature. Namely, Freud observed that *some* fathers and *some* father figures become threatened by their own sons. That is, they fear being supplanted by their sons, and so they grow to hate them.

This only happens when there's an excessive root of pride and insecurity in the father figure's heart. The absence of such pride and insecurity is what separates those spiritual fathers who become proud of their sons from those who grow to despise them.

Regrettably, some mentors suffer from both an inferiority complex and a superiority complex at the same time. Their shaky sense of identity cuts in both directions. In such cases, they become masters at the fine art of denial.

Caution: If you're a person who will one day mentor others, I have a sobering warning. If your ego hasn't been annihilated by the cross of Jesus Christ, you will end up becoming a Saul in the lives of those who are just as (or more) gifted than you are. And when God begins to elevate them in His service, you will go insane.

You'll become another sad example of lions eating their young. And as with every modern Saul, God's favor and anointing will leave you and be given to another. As Peter said,

> *God resists the proud, but gives grace to the humble.*
> *(1 Peter 5:5 NKJV)*

Saint John of the Cross warned Christians to be very careful whom they chose to be their mentors, for, in his words, "as the master so is the disciple; as the father so is the child."[1]

To my mind, one cannot show genuine respect for one's mentor by perpetuating his shortcomings and flaws.

Every father should be extremely proud of the son who surpasses him. True mentors freely give what they have to their spiritual sons and hope that their sons will exceed them. False mentors use their sons to increase their fame and carry on their legacies, and they become infuriated whenever their sons share their glory.

(2) Constructing Fellowship Tests

Those who are captured by the same spirit they oppose tend to create explicit or implicit "fellowship tests," which end up excluding genuine members of the body of Christ. A "test of fellowship" is a belief or practice that people employ as a gauge to determine if another person is worthy of their complete fellowship. Let me illustrate.

When I was sixteen, I was baptized in water to confess my faith and allegiance to Jesus Christ. Some years later, I joined a movement (or a "nondenominational" denomination) that told me that I had to be baptized in *their* church because any other baptism was null and void.

This "denomination" refused to recognize my former baptism simply because they had the elitist viewpoint that they exclusively had the corner on genuine baptism. Baptism was a "fellowship test" for them. Unless a Christian was baptized in *their* church, that Christian would always be viewed as second class.

Years later, I spent some time with a movement that carried this same spirit. For them, however, baptism wasn't their fellowship test. It was something else. Essentially, they believed that unless you were part of *their* particular movement, any experience of church life you had was meaningless. And they were terribly disinterested in hearing anything about it.

You had to be part of *their* movement in order to have a valid spiritual experience. And if you didn't, you were regarded as second class. To their minds, only they and their tiny movement were the divine custodians of true spiritual experience, both corporate and individual.

For me, it was déjà vu. It was the same song that the "we are the gatekeepers of authentic baptism" people had sung, only to a different tune. It reminded me of the rebuke that Jesus leveled to His disciples when they began to entertain the same sort of elitist mentality:

> *"Master," said John, "we saw a man driving out demons in your name and we tried to stop him, because he is not one of us." "Do not stop him," Jesus said, "for whoever is not against you is for you." (Luke 9:49–50)*

Note the words "we tried to stop him, *because he is not one of us.*"

The Corinthians were not alone in their tendency to create a "we are of Christ" party (1 Cor. 1:12–13).

There's nothing new in any of this. You can find it on the earth today in thousands of movements and denominations. It's like the saying goes: "It's the same song, third verse; could be better, but it's gonna get worse." And that song is commonly sung among those who have been captured by the same spirit they oppose.

It's my strong feeling that a genuine revelation of *the fullness of Christ* will strip you and me of all exclusiveness and sectarianism. And it will demolish an elitist attitude.

Think about what seeing Jesus Christ did to Paul of Tarsus. It transformed him from a religious, bigoted, sectarian, elitist Pharisee to someone who welcomed and embraced heathen Gentiles—the very people he was taught to despise all his life.

Paul's sighting of Christ annihilated a bigot and created an apostle.

If we see only *a part* of Christ and build a monument around that "sighting," then we are ripe for embracing an elitist spirit. But if we stay open to the whole Christ, looking for Him in other places, people, and movements, elitism will not find a home in us.

(3) Deifying a Unique Contribution

Those who are captured by the same spirit they oppose tend to make their unique contribution more important than Jesus Christ Himself. One can talk a great deal about Jesus Christ, and even about the need for knowing Him, and yet betray Him by one's actions and attitudes toward those who are His.

One of the most sobering passages of Scripture is where Jesus makes the statement that if a person rejects one of His disciples, they are rejecting Jesus Himself (Matt. 10:40; Luke 10:6).

Every church tradition, movement, and denomination has a valid contribution to make to the body of Christ. Some more than others, for sure. But there's great danger in making our contributions about Christ more important than Christ Himself.

(4) Refusing Diversity

Those who are captured by the same spirit they oppose refuse to live with diversity in their movement. Everyone in the group must rehearse the same party line. Those who do not are viewed with suspicion. They are either overtly silenced or excommunicated and shunned.

When diversity is forbidden in a group, it creates a "walking on eggshells" situation. People are not free to share what they *really* feel or believe. Legitimate concerns are swept under the rug. Rushes to judgment are routinely made, and the faintest hint of diverse thinking is viewed as subversive. (Note that I'm not speaking here of judging motives, being critical, and having a spirit of faultfinding. I'm speaking of legitimate concerns that are rooted in reality.)

Some group leaders use explicit tactics like overt threats to intimidate those who have valid concerns. Others use the vindictive weapon of public ridicule to belittle, demean, and insult them. This is a gutless way of evading an issue by seeking to make its victim the butt of contempt in a public forum.

Instead of dealing with the issue maturely and graciously in Christ, one uses ridicule to strike at another person and humiliate them in front of others in juvenile fashion. (Incidentally, those who feel they need to ridicule others have very low self-esteem. Vitriol is an effective way to hide one's own insecurities.)

Schoolyard belittling, juvenile taunting, and blue-blooded mockery are all tools of the flesh. And those who wield them smell of flesh. They grieve the Spirit of God and betray the spirit of the Lamb. And we have not so learned Jesus Christ.

I've watched this sort of behavior poison many relationships. The "cheap shot" that gets a laugh is the fleshly instrument of the insecure leader. Consequently, those who relish mocking others only reveal serious interior problems that they've never dealt with. Jealousy and envy are chief among them.

Even so, those who are captured by the same spirit they oppose cannot abide diversity. Instead of embracing it as a mark of fullness, they do all they can to squash it. And ridicule—a tool of the old man wielded by self-indulgent souls—is one way that it's accomplished.

(5) Embracing Self-Righteousness

Self-righteousness lies at the taproot of those who are captured by the same spirit they oppose. Self-righteousness is the attitude that makes one believe that they are more righteous, more holy, and more spiritual than others. It's an attribute of the flesh. The Pharisees of Jesus' day had PhDs in it. And for that reason, our Lord leveled the strongest words against them.

You can spot self-righteousness in a person pretty easily. Whenever people are quick to condemn others but excuse themselves, they are being self-righteous. Whenever they evaluate their mistakes and short-comings as being "less severe" than those of others, they are being self-righteous. Whenever they are blind to their own flaws but concern themselves with the flaws of others, they are being self-righteous.

There's only one Person in the universe who has the right to be self-righteous. And He isn't.

The Lord Jesus hates self-righteousness, plain and simple. The truth is, we are all unrighteous in ourselves. Our only righteousness is Christ. Who, then, can boast about that?[2]

All told: As the wind of God's Spirit blows on His body today, may He mercifully keep us from being captured by the same spirit we oppose.

CHAPTER 8

THE GOD OF UNSEEN ENDINGS

REVISING OUR SPIRITUAL EXPECTATIONS

The psalmist said that the Lord made known His *ways* to Moses but His *acts* to the children of Israel (Ps. 103:7). We have a God who doesn't do anything arbitrarily. He's quite deliberate in what He does.

It takes a lifetime to understand the ways of God. But the more we understand them, the more we understand who He is. For His ways give us insight into His character.

Each Christian has an expectation of who God is and how He should act under certain circumstances. When the Lord doesn't act according to our expectations, our faith gets tested. Some people are "offended" and fall away. Note the words of Jesus Himself about this.

> *Blessed is the man who does not fall away on account of me. (Luke 7:23)*

Here's the context behind those words. John the Baptist had just been put in a dark, cold prison. John's prison experience caused him to doubt that his cousin was in fact the Messiah. So John sent emissaries to Jesus, asking Him, "Are you the one who was to come, or should we expect someone else?" (Luke 7:19).

Jesus' reply to John comes straight from Isaiah 61: "Go back and report to John what you have seen and heard: The blind receive sight, the lame walk, those who have leprosy are cured, the deaf hear, the dead are raised, and the good news is preached to the poor. Blessed is the man who does not fall away on account of me."

Jesus, however, leaves out one very telling phrase from Isaiah 61, the one John would have expected to hear: *to proclaim freedom for the captives and release from darkness for the prisoners.*

John never left the prison.

"Blessed are those who do not fall away from Me, especially when I do not meet their expectations."

He Takes Away the First to Establish the Second

Along this same line, there's a passage of Scripture that sheds light on one of the ways in which God works, especially when He doesn't seem to follow through with what we think He's promised. It's found in Hebrews 10:9 (NASB):

> *He takes away the first in order to establish the second.*

In this text, the writer of Hebrews is discussing the old covenant. He points out that God took away the old covenant to establish the new. God took away all the ceremonies and sacrifices of the old covenant to establish the new covenant embodied in Jesus Christ. Jesus is the reality of everything in the old covenant. Christ is the real lamb, the real sacrifice, the real priest, and the real temple.

The writer goes on to say that God takes away the first covenant to establish the second, and the second covenant is better than the first. Note the principle: *God takes away to establish, and what He establishes is always better than what He takes away.*

For this reason, the word *better* is used thirteen times throughout the book of Hebrews (NASB). Christians have a better sacrifice, a better hope, a better tabernacle, a better priesthood, a better covenant, and better promises than what the old covenant provided.

"He takes away that He might establish" is a principle that governs one of the chief ways that God works with His people.

Evening and Morning

Let's trace this principle throughout the Bible. Return with me to the creation of the earth. When God created the planet, it was formless and void, and darkness covered the waters. After the darkness, God said, "Let there be light." Notice that the darkness preceded the light.

This establishes an important principle. When God begins something new, He always starts with darkness rather than light. First the darkness, then the light.

God then begins to create life-forms on the earth. The Scripture says, "And there was evening, and there was morning—the first day.... And there was evening, and there was morning—the second day.... And there was evening, and there was morning—the third day," and on and on until the seventh day.

Notice that the evening comes first. God's day starts with darkness, not light. It begins with evening, not morning. And when the seventh day arrives, God rests. The Scripture does not say, "And there was evening, and there was morning—the seventh day." On the seventh day, there is no evening and no morning mentioned. We are simply told that God ended His work and rested on that day.

Now what caused God to rest? The answer: humanity. God saw His image in the earth. Behold, I show you a mystery. *When God sees His image in the earth, He can rest.*

So God's beginnings start with evening. What we call the end of the day, God calls the beginning. In fact, every life-form begins in darkness. There are nine months of darkness for a human, and then the human sees light. At night when we are asleep, our bodies are resting and restoring, but we are unaware of it until morning. To put it another way, God's beginnings are our nights. And what we call the end, He calls the beginning.

Consequently, what may appear to be the end for you is the beginning for God. Our day starts out in the morning with birds chirping, newspapers thrown on the lawn, and fresh coffee percolating. But God's work begins in the evening. It begins with darkness. So we touch an important principle here. God takes away to establish, and what He establishes is always better. He takes away the darkness to establish the light. He takes away the evening to establish the morning.

In the Life of Job

Consider Job. Here is a man who experienced a dark night beyond telling. Job had great wealth, many friends, and many children. God had beautifully blessed him. And what happened?

God took it all away.

Job's dark night occurred suddenly without warning. An angel didn't send him an email saying, "Get ready, there's a big one coming!" God didn't send him a Tweet saying, "Look out, Job, you're going to lose everything in one day." No, there was no fax, email, or Twitter announcement.

It came without warning. In one day, Job lost his cattle, his crops, and his children. It appears that God went on vacation. This was Job's dark night. God was silent, but He wasn't absent. The Lord was present throughout the ordeal, from beginning to end. In fact, He was actually behind it—allowing it.

Job's drama was being played out on a double stage. Corresponding to what was happening on earth, there were things happening in the heavenly realm, all of which Job was completely unaware. Job was experiencing his evening, his darkness.

Let me remind you: The evening always has within it the promise of the morning. The night always has within it the promise of the day to come. When you go through the dark night, as a church or as an individual, remember that the morning is gestating, growing, and will eventually appear.

> *Weeping may endure for a night, but joy comes in the morning. (Ps. 30:5 NKJV)*

Job endured his evening. He was bombarded on every point to lose his faith in God—by pressure from his friends and his own wife. Yet Job maintained his integrity. His words are revealing: "The LORD gave and the LORD has taken away" (Job 1:21).

Yet after his evening—after his dark night—Job experienced his morning. God restored everything Job had lost and more. Job received double what was taken away (Job 42:10; James 5:11). He received more children. He received more wealth, more cattle, and more crops.

Not only that, but Job lived for 140 more years, and God blessed him during each one of those years.

I don't know about you, but whenever I read that account, I think to myself: *But what about those kids who are buried in Job's backyard?*

I have to believe that the Lord eased the pain and softened the memory somehow, and Job lived a peaceful, satisfied man the rest of his days. For comfort and peace are contained within the blessing of God.

Again: You and I have a God who takes away so that He may establish. And what He establishes is always better than what He took away.

In the Life of Joseph

Let's move forward in the biblical story. We come to Joseph the dreamer. Joseph was a young man who was part of a large family. He had a father who loved him very much.

One day, God gave Joseph a dream. In it, Joseph saw his destiny. And he was so excited that he began to brag about it to his brothers.

This turned out to be a profound mistake.

What happened? Joseph quickly entered into his dark night. His brothers threw him into a waterless pit—a place of darkness. And he was left there for dead. Not long after, Joseph was promoted to a prison and put on death row!

The psalmist says that the word of the Lord tried him as his soul fell into iron (Ps. 105:17–19). When Joseph was imprisoned, God's word was testing him to see whether or not he was going to let go of the vision or still cling to it despite his painful circumstances. Remarkably, Joseph held on to the vision all the way until the end, even though everything around him was contradicting him.

Joseph finally had his morning. God brought him out of the prison and exalted him to be ruler over Egypt. His family was restored. His brothers' hatred melted away into love. He regained what he had lost and received more than what the Lord had taken away.

Indeed, the vision had come to pass.

God takes away that He might establish, and what He establishes is always better.

In the Lives of Moses and Aaron

Enter now Moses and Aaron. These two men are leading the children of Israel in the wilderness. There arises a controversy over their leadership. Moses and Aaron are being challenged by some of God's people. God says to Moses, "I want you to take a rod from each of the leaders of the tribes of Israel—twelve rods. And I want you to put them in the tabernacle" (see Num. 17:1–4).

The rods were put in the Holy of Holies where only the high priest had access once a year. The Holy of Holies was the little room in the tabernacle where the presence of God rested on the ark of the covenant. The twelve rods were put behind the curtain in this room where there was no light. The only time that this room was lit up was when God's presence appeared on top of the ark of the covenant and He displayed His glory. At all other times, the room was utterly dark.

So the Lord says, "Take the rods and put them in the Holy of Holies in pure darkness for one whole night" (see Num. 17:5–8). That was an evening. That was darkness. That was a night. Then the morning came, and Moses took the rods out. Strikingly, one of them—Aaron's rod—had budded. Life came forth from a dead stick.

In the midst of the dark night, something was going on that no mortal could have ever imagined. In the morning, there was resurrection. The dead rod had produced blossoms.

Take note: Evening is the time of death. It's the time of hopelessness and helplessness. But the evening is always followed by the morning, and that's when resurrection occurs. Every evening holds the promise of the morning. Every night contains the promise of a new day. The Lord takes away that He might establish.

In the Life of David

David was a young boy in a seemingly functional family. Samuel, the heavyweight prophet of that time, selected David out of all the young men in the region. Samuel prophesied over David and anointed him to be king over all Israel. What a great vision and destiny.

What happened after that? *Nothing.* David was utterly ignored. Here he thought he was going to be a featured celebrity on TBN, have interviews with *Christianity Today*, and become a household name. Instead, nothing happened. Nothing at all.

Then, something did happen—Goliath. After David triumphed over Goliath and the Philistines, he attained instant popularity. People were singing the praises of David on the streets—until God chose to take his fame away. The next thing we learn about David is that he's in the wilderness being hunted like an animal by King Saul.

David has no friends, but he has more enemies than he can count. This was David's dark night. The evening had entered into his life, and it lasted a long time. You can read all about it in the Psalms. David is despairing everywhere. Yet after the dark night, God took away the first king, Saul, and He established the second king, David.

He took away the first that He might establish the second. And what He establishes is always better.

David was a better king than Saul. David's night was over. His evening had passed. Then came the morning and the light, and it was *very* good.

We have a Lord who always begins with evening. We have a God who begins in darkness. But He takes away so that He can establish. Look at Hosea 6:1–3:

> *Come, let us return to the LORD. He has torn us to pieces but he will heal us; he has injured us but he will bind up our wounds. After two days he will revive us; on the third day he will restore us, that we may live in his presence…. As surely as the sun rises, he will appear.*

What a beautiful passage. God tears us in order to heal us. He smites us in order to bind and revive us. Then on the third day, when the sun rises in the morning, He appears.

In the Life of Jesus

We come now to Jesus Christ. Think about our Lord's birth. When Jesus was born, darkness covered the earth. When Jesus made His appearance on this planet, Israel was under the iron fist of the Roman Empire. God's people were being oppressed and suppressed. It was a sad, dark time for the people of Israel. It was an evening, a dark night. And then the Light appeared.

> *In him was life, and that life was the light of men. The light shines in the darkness, but the darkness has not understood it.... The true light that gives light to every man was coming into the world. (John 1:4–5, 9)*

After living on the earth for thirty-three years, our Lord had a profoundly dark night in Gethsemane. It was there that He faced the reality of a gruesome, catastrophic evening that awaited Him at Calvary. But He submitted to it. The writer of Hebrews says that the Lord endured the cross for the joy that was set before Him (12:2). Jesus knew that a glorious morning would succeed His evening. He knew that the dawn would follow His dark night. This assurance gave Him the power to endure.

But look over at the disciples. That's another story altogether. I want to paint the scene for you. These are the associates of the Lord's ministry. The last three years have been cushy for them. They got their IRS taxes paid by going fishing. When they were hungry, the Lord created food out of scraps. They were insulated from criticism and persecution. Jesus handled it all. They simply followed and observed.

But Jesus forewarned the Twelve saying, "I will be taken away from you; but it is *better* that I be taken away. For if I am not taken away, the Spirit cannot come" (see John 14:2–4; 16:7–16).

Jesus told the disciples of John the Baptist, "My disciples do not fast when the Bridegroom is here. But when He is *taken away*, then they will fast and they will mourn" (see Mark 2:19–20).

The Lord was indeed taken away. And what was the disciples' response? They went back to their old life. I suspect they were thinking, *It's over. We followed Him for over three years, and He let them kill Him. So where are we now?*

The Lord forewarned that they would experience sorrow. But their sorrow would be turned to joy.

The cross occurred on Friday. But as the preacher of old said, "Watch out, Devil, 'cause yonder come Sunday morning!"

Yes, Sunday morning came. But Sunday morning is so far removed from Friday that it's hard to conceive. Sometimes there arc light-years between Friday and Sunday.

When we are enduring the dark night, we are not thinking about the morning. We are not thinking about the day. We can only see the blackness. Nevertheless, the morning will indeed come to pass, just as it did with our Lord.

A Woman in Labor

The Lord used a parable once about a woman who was in labor. Consider this woman. She is pregnant. She must acquire a new wardrobe. It matters not what she wears, she still feels fat. The curves have vanished. Now there are stretch marks. It doesn't matter how she sits, she still can't get comfortable. She can no longer wear her two-piece for the summer.

And then comes the labor. I have no idea how cataclysmic the pain must be. But I have heard the screams firsthand. Talk about darkness! Talk about pain! Talk about suffering!

But what did the Lord say about it? When the woman completes her travail and the baby is born, she remembers her pain no more (John 16:21). She forgets everything—even the nasty things that came out of her mouth while she was screaming. The memory is erased because a new child is born into the world, and the morning has come. The night is forgotten.

The disciples forgot this when their Lord was taken away from them. They experienced the dark night. Those three days must have seemed like an eternity for them. There was no hope on the horizon.

Recall the parable of the old wineskin and the new wineskin (Matt. 9:17). God will take away the old wineskin because it can't contain the new wine.

The Lord needs a new wineskin for our day. So He tampers with our wineskins. He wrecks them if He wishes. He destroys the old wineskin so that He can hand us a new wineskin. That's why there are so many changes today in the body of Christ. The

Lord wants to deposit His new wine. And the new wine is always *better* than the old wine.

This is the way in which our Lord works. First the evening, then the morning. First death, then life. First the night, then the light.

What you and I call the end of the day, God calls the beginning.

So when you walk into your dark night, just remember: "This too shall pass." All afflictions have an expiration date (2 Cor. 4:17).

The First Born and the Second Born

All throughout Scripture, God's choice is always with the second born, not the first born. Adam had two sons: Cain and Abel. Cain was the first born, and Abel was the second. God took Cain away and put His favor on Abel.

Abraham's first born was Ishmael. God took Ishmael away, and put His favor on Isaac, the second born.

Isaac had two sons: Esau and Jacob. "Jacob have I loved. Esau have I hated." Esau was the first born; Jacob was the second. God rejected Esau to establish Jacob.

Joseph had two sons: Manasseh and Ephraim. Manasseh was the first born; Ephraim was the second. God rejected Manasseh and put His favor on Ephraim.

David had a firstborn son with Bathsheba, and God literally took him away. But the second born was Solomon, and God gave the kingdom to him.

When the Lord judged Egypt, the last plague that fell upon the nation was the death of all the firstborn sons. The second-born sons were not in danger.

Why does God reject the first born and favor the second born?

Paul gives us a clue in 1 Corinthians 15:46–47:

> *The spiritual did not come first, but the natural,*
> *and after that the spiritual. The first man was of*
> *the dust of the earth, the second man from heaven.*

God took away the first man, Adam, and put him out of his misery. He then established the second man, Jesus Christ (Rom. 5—6; 1 Cor. 15:20–49).

Our first birth was a birth into Adam. We inherited his nature and incurred his judgment. So God rejects our first birth. It is our second birth—our new birth into Christ—our birth from above that God accepts.

Summary

Dear Christian, the Lord will never meet *all* your expectations. Sometimes He will; other times He will not. But He is always in control, and He does all things well (Mark 7:37; Rom. 8:28).

Consequently, when you are going through the dark night,

remember: It's not the end. It's only the beginning. As high as God is going to elevate you is as deep as He digs to lay the foundation.

There is a spiritual principle that the Lord never gives anything, but that He first allows it to be lost. Jesus said that until you lose something, you can't really have it (Matt. 16:25; Luke 6:38). God gives something first, then allows it to be taken away, that it may be given again. This is the principle of death and resurrection, and it is repeated all throughout Scripture. Ever notice all of those *re-* terms in the Bible: *restoration, regeneration, restitution, recreation, rebirth, renewal, resurrection, revive,* etc.?

Our Lord is a God of restoration. He takes away the first to establish the second. And the second is always better.

The Hebrew day begins at sunset. Life always begins in the dark—the darkness of a womb. Early church tradition says that Jesus was born in a cave of darkness which served as a stable. Our Lord died upon a cross and "darkness came over the whole land" (Mark 15:33). He rose again from the dead "while it was still dark" (John 20:1).

So get behind the eyes of your Lord and remember how He works. It is in the hidden hours of the night that God does His deepest work of transformation. The night, the evening, and the darkness are all promises of a new day. If you can hold this in your heart, it will change your life.

CHAPTER 9

STRIPPING DOWN TO CHRIST ALONE

REVISING THE HOLY SPIRIT'S MINISTRY

I'm often asked what I believe about "the gifts of the Spirit." My typical answer is that I believe in them—all of them. However, I believe in and practice them *without* the classic Charismatic packages and Pentecostal wrappings.

A large chunk of my Christian life was spent in Charismatic circles. I benefited from being in those circles, and through them God taught me a great deal about the supernatural workings of His Spirit.

However, many years ago, I came into an experience of the

Spirit's power that looked nothing like what I had seen in any Charismatic or Pentecostal church to which I had belonged. For me, it was a new experience of the Spirit; one that was less artificial, less contrived, and less centered on the Spirit Himself. Rather, it was an experience that was authentic, pure, and centered on the Lord Jesus Christ.

For this reason, I'm neither a cessationist (a person who believes that some spiritual gifts have ceased) nor a Charismatic (one who emphasizes spiritual gifts). Instead, I consider myself to be *post-Charismatic*.

Note that what I'm about to write is based on my experience in the Pentecostal/Charismatic Movement. Your experience may differ.

Post-Charismatic

I believe John Wimber was the first to use this term. Lee Grady, editor of *Charisma* magazine, estimated that in 1990 there were as many as ninety-two million people who described themselves as post-Charismatic. In more recent times, author Rob McAlpine has written thoughtfully on the subject.[1] Thus, I owe parts of my definition of "post-Charismatic" to Wimber and McAlpine.

When I say that I'm post-Charismatic (or neo-Charismatic), I mean the following:

- I believe that the authentic gifts of the Holy Spirit are still operative in the church today. Not only do I believe in them, but I've also experienced them. However, I also believe that the artificial wrappings that have been attached to them should be discarded, for they distract us from Christ.

- I believe that being "Spirit-filled" cannot be narrowly defined to refer exclusively to those people who have demonstrated one particular spiritual gift at some particular point in their lives. On that score, I had a particular experience with the Holy Spirit in 1983. Some would say that I was "filled with the Spirit" because of it. However, I would argue that I was filled with the Spirit before then as well as many times afterward (see Acts 2:4; 4:8, 31; 9:17; 13:9, 52; Eph. 5:18–20).

- I've grown tired of the excesses and abuses that many modern Charismatics have fallen prey to in both practice and teaching. These excesses and abuses go back to when the movement was spawned. It's one of the birth defects with which Pentecostalism was born.[2]

- I'm against humanly engineered hype and pulpit showmanship and calling it "the moving of the Spirit." Perhaps you've seen this before. You pour in the right prayers, sing the right songs with the right fervor, turn the crank, and out comes "the Spirit's moving."

- I'm leery of "personal prophecies" that justify ridiculous practices and ludicrous decisions and fly in the face of Spirit-inspired wisdom.

- I cast a skeptical eye on the exaggerated and sometimes fabricated stories of the miraculous. That includes the puffing up of numbers when healings or saved souls are calculated. (I've discovered that if a Pentecostal/Charismatic reports a figure of souls saved or sicknesses healed, you might be wise to cut it in half and divide by two to get the actual number.)

- I stand opposed to the elitist attitude conveyed by some who purport to possess spiritual gifts.

- I'm opposed to forcing the exercise of spiritual gifts on God's people.

- I'm against those doctrines that promote seeking wealth and material prosperity from God at the expense of caring for the poor and relieving the sufferings of the oppressed.

- I'm opposed to the idea that spiritual transformation *normally* takes place in onetime miraculous encounters rather than by a long-term process of being conformed to Christ's image by the instrument of His cross. (Transformation does not occur without suffering.)

- I'm against using the Holy Spirit and His gifts to make human beings the center of the universe.

- I'm against promoting an intoxication with the restoration of the gifts of the Spirit. (The only thing worth being intoxicated with is Jesus Christ.)

- I'm critical of the legalism that was injected into the bloodstream of the Pentecostal movement and that later infiltrated the Charismatic mind.

- I'm profoundly skeptical of any activity—natural or supernatural—that claims to be a work of the Holy Spirit if it doesn't bring attention to the Lord Jesus.

- I believe that the real fruit of prayer is not spiritual insight, spiritual revelation, or spiritual encounter, but the transformation of character. To my mind, the product of real prayer is what Ignatius of Loyola called the *instrumentum conjunctum cum Deo*—an instrument shaped to the contours of the hand of God.

- I believe that spiritual maturity is not the ability to see the extraordinary, but the ability to see the ordinary through God's eyes. Consequently, no matter how wonderful our experience or encounter with God is, the test of its worth is in the fruit it bears in our lives and the lives of others.

All told, I believe in the supernatural operation of the Holy Spirit but without the classic Charismatic and Pentecostal trappings and wrappings. A great deal of those wrappings are artificial, learned by imitation, and detract from the reality and primacy of Jesus Christ. So while I'm post-Charismatic, I'm certainly not post–Holy Spirit.

Restoring the Spirit's Undefiled Work

If we need a restoration of the Holy Spirit today, it's a restoration of His pure and undefiled work. That's my conviction anyway.

So if I'm against all of the above, what am I for? I'm *for* the centrality, supremacy, sovereignty, and exaltation of the Lord Jesus. Period.

To my mind, the Holy Spirit has but one job: to reveal, to make known, to magnify, to glorify, and to make central and supreme the Lord Jesus Christ.

The following is a revealing quote by Frank Bartleman. Bartleman was part of the Azusa Street revival that gave birth to the modern Pentecostal/Charismatic Movement in the early 1900s. I believe Bartleman spoke ahead of his time. He foresaw the dangers of co-opting Jesus Christ by putting the Holy Spirit on the throne. He wrote,

> *In the beginning of the Pentecostal work, I became very much exercised in the Spirit that Jesus should not be slighted, "lost in the temple," by the exaltation of the Holy Ghost and of the gifts of the Spirit. There seemed to be a great danger of losing sight of the fact that Jesus was "all in all." I endeavored to keep Him as the central theme and figure before His people. Jesus will always be the center of our preaching. All comes*

*through and in Him. The Holy Spirit was given to
"show the things of Christ." The work of Calvary, the
atonement, must be the center for our consideration.
The Holy Ghost will never draw our attention from
Christ to Himself, but rather reveal Christ in a fuller
way. We are in the same danger today.*

*There is nothing deeper nor higher than to
know Christ. Everything is given by God to that
end. The "one Spirit" is given to that end. Christ
is our salvation and our all. That we might know
"the breadth, and length, and depth, and height of
the love of Christ" (Ephesians 3:18–19), "having a
spirit of wisdom and revelation in the knowledge
of Him" (Ephesians 1:17). It was "to know Him
(Christ)," for which Paul strove.… We may not
even hold a doctrine, or seek an experience, except
in Christ. Many are willing to seek power from
every battery they can lay their hands on in order
to perform miracles, draw attention and adoration
of the people to themselves, thus robbing Christ of
His glory and making a fair showing in the flesh.…
Religious enthusiasm easily goes to seed. The human
spirit so predominates the show-off, religious spirit.
But we must stick to our text—Christ. He alone can*

save. The attention of the people must first of all,
and always, be held to Him…. Any work that exalts
the Holy Ghost or the gifts of the Spirit above Jesus
will finally end up in fanaticism. Whatever causes
us to exalt and love Jesus is well and safe. The reverse
will ruin all. The Holy Ghost is a great light, but
will always be focused on Jesus for His revealing.[3]

Being "Spirit-Filled"

One of the first churches I ever planted taught me a great lesson on this score. Their meetings were open, participatory, and indelibly centered on Jesus Christ. They had no building, no clergy, and no set order of worship.

Each member would share his or her experience and insight into Christ as a result of seeking Him the week before. The church had a steady flux of visitors. Most of these visitors would remark, "All you talk about is Christ. You seem to have a deep experience of the indwelling of Jesus."

One particular Sunday, two men visited the church. When the meeting was over, they sat with some of the members and asked, "How come you guys don't ever talk about the Holy Spirit? All you talk about is Christ."

One of our young men in his early twenties answered with

wisdom that exceeded his years: "Well, maybe it's because the Holy Spirit only speaks about one thing—*Jesus Christ.*"

I was not present for that meeting. The story was rehearsed to me. But it's one I shall never forget.

If you want to know if a person is full of the Holy Spirit, listen to his words and watch his life. As far as his words go, he'll have one central focus. It will be Christ. And his life will match his words. He won't be perfect by any means. Nor will he be above making mistakes. But he will exhibit a spirit of kindness, honesty, and an inclusive openness to all of God's children—the outstanding marks of Christ's character.

Awhile back a friend of mine was perplexed about a certain minister whom he sat under for years. He said, "Frank, I don't understand. This man's message was Christ-centered. He talked a lot about Christ. But as I got to know him personally, I discovered that behind closed doors he lied constantly, he was always jealous of other people whom God blessed and anointed; he was astonishingly arrogant, sectarian, highly egotistical, and rewrote history to put others in a bad light. In public, he ridiculed and demeaned others subtly. He hurt many people, even though he preached passionately against hurting Christians. I just don't understand it."

My response was simple. A person is not Christ-centered or Spirit-filled just because they preach the centrality of Christ. If they contradict the nature of Jesus by their character (their consistent, patterned behavior), they are *not* Christ-centered or full of the Spirit despite the rhetoric they parade.

An Invaluable Lesson

Let me pass on a word of advice. If you ever hit a fork in the road with the people with whom you do church (whatever that looks like), there's one sure way that the Lord can get what He wants. Drop whatever is causing the problem, and let it *go into death.*

There is nothing for us to cling to except the Lord Jesus Christ. Nothing. So let that other thing that is causing division go into death. Give it up, and watch what the Lord can do.

This is the principle of death and resurrection. Whenever we place something into death, if it was born of Christ to begin with, it will return again. It will come forth out of the ground. But when it comes forth, it will always look different from what it looked like before it died.

Everything looks different in resurrection.

A group of Christians I was a part of did this very thing with respect to our initial differences about the Holy Spirit. Some of the group believed in spiritual gifts and practiced them in Pentecostal/ Charismatic fashion. The other group members didn't believe in the gifts (they were cessationists). We all decided to lay down our view of spiritual gifts at the feet of the cross. We let them *go into death.*

The result was remarkable. In time, the gifts of the Spirit began operating in a very natural, unassuming way. There was no grandstanding or bluster. It was truly organic—out of life. The gifts didn't look Pentecostal, Charismatic, or non-Pentecostal/Charismatic. All the old wrappings had vanished. This was a work of the Spirit that was fresh and new. We had learned the lesson of stripping down to Christ alone.

I believe the Lord desires to revise the work of His Spirit in the lives of many of His children today. It may involve death to practices or beliefs we've held dear. But where there is no death, there is no resurrection.

CHAPTER 10

YOUR CHRIST IS TOO SMALL

REVISING OUR CHIEF PURSUIT

The promise of the new covenant is thus:

> *I will put My laws in their mind and write them on their hearts; and I will be their God, and they shall be My people. None of them shall teach his neighbor, and none his brother, saying, "Know the LORD," for all shall know Me, from the least of them to the greatest of them. For I will be merciful to their unrighteousness, and their sins and their*

lawless deeds I will remember no more. (Heb. 8:10–12 NKJV)

Note the words "all shall know Me." This is the beating heart of God.

To know the Lord is at the heart of the gospel. Knowing the Lord is eternal life (John 17:3). It was the plea of the prophet (Hos. 6:3) and the passion of Paul's life (Phil. 3:10). Yet how often do we hear this talked about today?

I'll be blunt: Either you and I can know God intimately, or the gospel is a sham. One of the rewards of our Lord's suffering is that we *all* shall know Him … "from the least to the greatest."

We know God in the face of Jesus Christ. But the truth is, we can't fully know Christ as an individual. We may only know Him fully through the new creation. That is, *we know Him through His body* (2 Cor. 5:16–17).

This particular understanding changed everything for me as a young Christian. My life was revolutionized when I realized that my brothers and sisters in Christ are *parts* of Christ; therefore, I had to learn how to listen to my Lord *through* them.

I also discovered that the Lord is *constantly* speaking. He speaks to us inwardly, through circumstances as well as through His own people—even at times when we are unaware of it.

If this is true (and I assure you it is), then how well we know the Lord depends on how sensitive we are and how connected we are to the other parts of His body.

My Journey into Community

My journey into Christian community taught me that the Christian life, in its core essence, is living by *another* life. It's living by Christ (John 6:57 KJV; Gal. 2:20; Col. 3:4). Yet it's not simply living only by the Lord who indwells me. It's also a matter of living by the Lord who indwells my Christian brothers and sisters.

I live by the Lord who lives in me, and I live by the Lord who lives in my fellow brethren (in whom Christ also dwells). God has designed it that way. Consequently, if we will know our Lord deeply, we must be connected to other members of His body in a concrete way. And it doesn't hurt at all to include in that mix exposure to the great teachers of the past whom God gifted to reveal Christ to His church.

Throughout my Christian life, I've met believers who had their own private walks with the Lord. They never knew Christian community, yet they had an extremely strong devotional life. Every person who fit that bill was lopsided in some arena of their lives. The reason? They didn't avail themselves of the balancing and tempering of the body.

No Christian is wired to live an individualistic Christian life. Without Christian community, we cannot grow normally in

Christ. We were designed to live with other believers and receive their spiritual portion. If you doubt this, please read 1 Corinthians 12 with this possibility in mind.

The First Seeing of Christ

When we first meet the Lord, He makes Himself quite irresistible to us. He wins us over with His charm. He conquers our hearts with His unconditional love. He draws us near to Himself by His passion, and we fall in love.

If we come into a higher vision of His purpose, we get connected with other believers. We then begin to know Him with others. We pursue Christ corporately.[1]

But there is a danger in receiving a greater revelation of the Lord Jesus Christ, one that moves from shallow waters into the depths. It's the peril of allowing our *first* seeing of Christ to shape the way we recognize Him for the rest of our lives. (Please read that sentence again.)

I'm going to make this shockingly pointed: *The Lord Jesus Christ will end up coming to us in a way that makes it easy for us to reject Him.*

If we are pressing on to know the Lord, He will eventually come to us in a way that makes it easy for us to ignore Him, dismiss Him, and even reject Him. I've watched this happen repeatedly among Christian groups that felt they had a corner on knowing the Lord.

I believe this is God's way of keeping us humble and open, like a child.

Jesus Christ is the same yesterday, today, and forever (Heb. 13:8). Do you recall the way He came into the earth?

Consider the situation. For centuries, Israel had waited for a political Messiah. They expected Him to break the yoke of Roman bondage and liberate God's people from Roman oppression.

But how did the Messiah make His entrance into the world? He came in a way that made it easy for His own people to reject Him. He entered the planet as a frail baby, born in a feeding room for animals. The King of the universe was born as a weak human being in the ill-starred town of Bethlehem, in the midst of the stain and stench of animal manure. And His parents? A poor Jewish couple.

There He was. The promised Messiah who was expected to overthrow the mighty Roman Empire and set Israel free from Gentile oppression. A needy Nazarene born in a manger.

Ironically, none of the Bible scholars who had the Old Testament memorized and knew the prophecies about the Messiah's coming were present at Christ's birth. The only people who were present were those who were led to Bethlehem by revelation. All of them happened to be shepherds and pagan astrologers, not Bible scholars.

When Jesus grew up, He ate and drank in their presence and

taught in their streets (Luke 13:26). Yet they didn't recognize who He was. He was unassumingly modest, of humble origin. A mere craftsman, the son of a craftsman.

He grew up in the despised city of Nazareth, fraternizing with the despised and oppressed. But more startling, He befriended sinners (Luke 7:34). As such, the people of God didn't recognize Him. Why? Because He came in a way that made it easy for them to reject Him.

And what about the disciples? Read the story again. Jesus continued to break out of their expectations. He couldn't be pinned down, figured out, or boxed in. The Twelve were constantly confounded by Him. His teachings were offensive. His actions scandalous. His reactions baffling.

But the greatest offense of all was the cross. It offended everyone—both Jew and Gentile. The only crown the promised Messiah-King would accept was a crown of thorns. Look at Him again. A suffering Messiah, a defeated King. Boy, it's easy to reject Him.

One of the Lord's most faithful disciples teaches us this principle well. Mary Magdalene was the first person to see the resurrected Christ. Do you remember what she did as soon as she recognized Him? She grabbed Him, and she wouldn't stop clinging to Him.

Jesus responded, "Stop clinging to me" (see John 20:17).[2]

Why did Jesus tell Mary to stop clinging to Him? Because He had somewhere to go. He was on the move. Jesus was poised to go to Galilee to see the other disciples and then to ascend to His Father.

Note the principle: He was moving forward, but she was clinging to Him.

Jesus was in effect saying to her: "Mary, stop holding on to Me. There's a new way to know Me that's different from what you've experienced thus far. Let Me go, for I must move on."

A Vanishing God

Do you remember the disciples who walked on the road to Emmaus? Their hopes were shattered by the Lord's horrible death. Suddenly, the resurrected Christ began walking beside them, yet their eyes were blinded from recognizing Him.

However, when He engaged in the very simple gesture of breaking bread (something He had done frequently before them), their eyes were opened.

He then quickly disappeared from their sight.

These stories hold a critical insight. You cannot cling to the Christ you know today. He will vanish from your midst. Jesus Christ is an elusive Lover. Seeking Him is a progressive engagement that never ends. He doesn't dance to our music. He doesn't sing to our tune.

Perhaps He will in the beginning when He woos us to Himself, but that season will eventually end. And just when you think you've laid hold of Him, He will slip out of your grasp. He will appear to you as a stranger. But upon second glance, we'll soon discover that He's no stranger at all. Emmaus will be repeated.

We all wish to cling to the Lord that we know *now*. We all wish to hold on to the Christ that has been revealed to us *today*. But mark my words: He will come to us in a way that we do not expect—through people who we're prone to ignore and inclined to write off.

Perhaps they don't talk our religious language. Perhaps they aren't theologically sophisticated. Perhaps they don't use our vocabulary. Perhaps they don't share our jargon or parrot our religious idioms.

And so we cling fast to the Lord that we recognize—receiving only those who talk our language, use our jargon, and employ our catchphrases—and all along we end up turning the Lord Jesus Christ away.

I have watched this happen repeatedly. Both among Christians who gather in traditional churches as well as among those who gather outside of them.

What, then, does our Lord do when we fail to receive Him when He comes to us in an unexpected way? *He moves on.* And the revelation that we have of Him ceases to grow.

I've seen churches and movements stop dead in the water,

living off a revelation of Christ that was delivered to them twenty or thirty years ago. And they never moved beyond it.

In fact, this is the very root of denominationalism and Christian movements. It works like this: A group of Christians sees an important aspect of Christ. That insight usually comes from a servant of the Lord whom God has raised up to restore a certain truth to His church. The group is captured by it. Even changed by it. And they stand on the earth to promote and express it.

But then, subtly, they build a circle around it. And then a castle and a wall. They then enshrine it. And when someone else comes in contact with them with another aspect of Christ to share, they blow it off with monumental disinterest.

Why? Because it's different from the original sighting of the Lord that they received.

In effect, the group refuses to have complete fellowship with other Christians who are not like them.

Please don't misunderstand. Fellowship is not having a meal with somebody. *Fellowship is mutual participation and exchange.* It's a two-way street. If you and I have fellowship, that means that I receive what the Lord has given you and that you receive what the Lord has given me. And we are both enriched. *That's fellowship.*

Allow me to confess: If I only fellowshipped with those whose beliefs matched mine, then, right now, I couldn't have fellowship with myself fifteen years ago! Furthermore, twenty years ago I would have had to excommunicate my current self from the kingdom of God!

Jesus Christ is richer, larger, and more glorious than any of us could ever imagine. And He comes to us in ways that make it tempting to reject Him.

When Peter, James, and John saw the transfigured Lord on the holy mountain, Peter wanted to build a tabernacle for Jesus, Moses, and Elijah and remain on the mountain to enjoy the encounter. But God would not allow it (Matt. 17:1–13).

There is something in our fallen nature that, like Peter, wishes to build a monument around a spiritual encounter with God and remain there. But the Lord will not have it. He will always break free from our frail attempts to pin Him down, box Him up, and hold Him in place. And He does so by coming to us in new and unexpected ways.

Fearing Diversity

Many Christians fear diversity. We all love unity, but we tend toward uniformity. This tendency is most clearly seen in denominationalism. But it exists vibrantly outside of denominational lines as well.

Diversity, however, is part of the nature of the body of Christ. It's also woven into the universe. Look at creation. Look at your physical body. Look at the eternal Trinity who brought both into existence. What do you find? Particularity with unity. Diversity with harmony.

Point: Diversity is a sign of fullness. Therefore, diversity should be embraced and not feared or rejected. Yet few things so test the human heart as does diversity.

(Obviously, I'm not suggesting that we embrace heretical ideas about Jesus Christ. I'm rather speaking about genuine Christian fellowship that is based on the New Testament revelation of Christ and echoed in the ancient creeds.)

In my early years as a Christian, some of the brothers in my fellowship held to a teaching that made "exercising faith" the central emphasis of the gospel. Their zeal for "living by faith" was not hidden by any means. It was proclaimed quite loudly. These brothers sought to persuade everyone else in the church to embrace their emphasis. And they were unhappy with any other insight or emphasis that didn't directly relate to theirs.

These men had made their particular insight into "faith" the whole ball of wax. And they wanted everyone else to conform to it. It was during those days that I learned that zealously emphasizing any particular truth, no matter how valid, and trying to persuade everyone else to embrace it was a money-back guarantee for a church split.

If I feel that the Lord has given me a particular insight into an important truth, I should not try to coerce everyone else to embrace it with the same passion that I do. A church should be free in this matter. Every believer is at liberty to embrace and share his or her understanding of Christ. However, a church will only grow properly when its members learn how to *incorporate* one another's insights into their overall understanding of the Lord.

Until our Lord returns, we will all continue to "see in a mirror, darkly" (1 Cor. 13:12 ASV). Consequently, a church ought to learn the fine art of weaving together the varied experiences and insights that each member brings to it. Those experiences and insights will be diverse. But they are what make up the body of Christ. And as long as they don't take away from the gospel or depart from the biblical revelation of Christ, they ought to be embraced.

Sometimes these experiences and insights will constitute a paradox. That is, they will appear to stand in contradiction to one another. For instance, some in the church may emphasize the sovereignty of God in all things. They will remind the church that all difficulties that come into our lives have first passed through the loving hands of God before they got to us. Therefore, they are for our good, and we ought to "submit to God" in them (James 4:7a; see also Rom. 8:28).

Others may emphasize that we are in a spiritual warfare and that we have an enemy who will attack us through the circumstances of life. In such cases, the Lord wishes for us to "resist the devil" so that he will flee from us (James 4:7b; see also 1 Peter 5:8–9).

So on the one hand, we should submit. But on the other, we should resist. Both are true. And both must be held in tension.

Throughout the years, I have come to see that the great bulk of divine truth is paradoxical. For this reason, I have learned to live in the presence of mystery, paradox, and spiritual contradiction. So much so that I can take a nap in the face of it.

Jesus Christ can be known, but He's also a mystery. (Col. 2:2). The incarnation is the "absolute paradox," as Kierkegaard put it. "Oh, the depth of the riches of the wisdom and knowledge of God! How unsearchable his judgments, and his paths beyond tracing out!" (Rom. 11:33).

The Dangers of New Insight

With every new seeing of the Lord, there is the temptation to become proud of that new seeing. There seems to be a subtle arrogance that seeks to seep into the human heart when one experiences a deeper experience or understanding of Christ.

Let me be clear. There is nothing more opposite of the Spirit of Jesus Christ than the spirit of pride and arrogance. A famous saying goes like this: It's possible to be "pure as angels and as proud as devils." I disagree. If you're proud, you're not pure. For God resists the proud (1 Peter 5:5; James 4:6).

We find Christ in only one issue: poverty. "Blessed are the poor in spirit," were our Lord's words (Matt. 5:3). A spirit of poverty says, "I need to know Him more. I don't have the corner on Him. I am a child in this business. I'm still in school. I'm still learning. I haven't arrived."

Here's a prayer worth praying. Whenever you see the Lord in a way that steals your breath, that's the time to turn to Him and say, "Lord, let me not lose touch. Keep my feet on the ground and cause me to always remember that I am no better than any other Christian."

For it is in times of great revelation that we need the humility of Christ the most. Recall Paul's thorn in the flesh. God put the thorn into his life to keep his feet on the ground in the face of extraordinary spiritual revelation (2 Cor. 12:7).

I have often reflected on the church in Ephesus. Paul lived in Ephesus for three years raising up a church. By his own testimony, he proclaimed "the whole counsel of God" to the believers there (Acts 20:27 NKJV).

Paul unveiled to the Ephesian believers the vision of God's eternal purpose for three years. He uncorked the mystery of God to them in great depths (Eph. 1—3; 6:19; Col. 1—2; 4:3).

Paul held meetings every day for five hours a day in a facility called the school of Tyrannus where he declared Christ and trained young workers.[3] Timothy, Titus, and six other men were present as his apprentices. I'm sure those young apprentices ministered to the Ephesian church as well.

After Paul was imprisoned, Timothy moved to Ephesus and ministered to the church there for a number of years. Some years later, the beloved disciple John ended up in Ephesus. Apollos, who was "mighty in the Scriptures," also spent time in Ephesus (Acts 18:24 NASB). So perhaps the church benefited from his ministry also.

Point: The church in Ephesus received the deepest and highest revelation of Christ through choice servants of God—Paul, John, Timothy, Titus, Apollos, etc. And yet, as the New Testament closes, we discover that the church in Ephesus was corrected by the Lord for leaving her first love (Rev. 2:1–4).

What happened? If experience has taught me anything, I would guess that they simply stopped pursuing Him. They got stuck. They clung to the Christ they had been given by the greatest servants of God, and they stopped there.

To put it another way, *their Christ was too small!*

I will close this chapter with a question: How well can you know the Lord? You can know Him in proportion to the poverty that's within your heart. "Blessed are the poor in spirit" (Matt. 5:3). The opposite of that statement is what the Laodicean church said of herself: "I am rich, have become wealthy, and have need of nothing" (Rev. 3:17 NKJV).

A sure mark of spiritual poverty is a wide heart. If you have a narrow heart, you will recognize Christ only through *some* of His people. And you will be blinded to find Him through others. Jesus Christ is a lot larger than what most of us have thought, and He works through a lot more people than we would expect.

In C. S. Lewis's *Prince Caspian*, Aslan tells Lucy, "Every year you grow, you will find Me bigger." This is a wonderful description of authentic spiritual growth. We know we are growing in the Lord when Jesus Christ is becoming bigger in our eyes.

Is your Christ too small? May we rescript our lives in a way that opens our hearts to the fullness of Jesus.

Please, Lord, revise us again.

AFTERWORD

THE THREE GOSPELS

Now to him who is able to establish you by my gospel and the proclamation of Jesus Christ.

—Romans 16:25

When it comes to the matter of living out the gospel, most believers can be divided up into two camps: the libertines and the legalists.

Here is a description of the libertines: They have accepted Jesus as their Savior. They go to church, own a Bible, and believe in God. However, they appear to have no vital relationship with the Lord. In addition, they hold to many of the same values as non-Christians.

If you were to examine their lifestyle, you would discover the behavior of libertines to be scarcely different from non-Christians. Their attitude is that God wants us to believe in Him, be nice to others, and try our best to be good. Beyond that, the Almighty doesn't particularly care how we live. So long as a person mentally assents that God exists and Jesus is Savior, they are worthy to bear the name "Christian."

The libertine is a product of a certain kind of gospel. Note that I am using the word *gospel* in a very specific sense to describe one's message about Christ and the Christian life (Rom. 2:16; 16:25; 2 Tim. 2:8). I am not using it in the more general sense to describe the gospel story as it is presented in the New Testament (Mark 1:1).

In broad strokes, the gospel of libertinism can be described as follows: Believing in Jesus is intellectual assent to certain faith propositions. God has little interest in the way people live their lives; He simply expects us to do the best we can. Believing in Jesus has little impact on a person's lifestyle or values. It's more of a privatized intellectual belief system. Here are some libertine statements:

> "We are all sinners, and we all sin. God understands."

"The Bible isn't completely relevant for us today. We can't expect to hold to the same values as people did in biblical times. We live in a different world with different values."

"I live the way I want. God loves me, and I am saved, so I can do anything I please."

"Yes, I'm a Christian. But regarding my sin, that's just the way I was made. I don't want to change, I can't change, and I won't change."

The gospel of libertinism is aimed primarily at the flesh. Its message gives the fallen nature free rein to do whatever, whenever it pleases. At the same time, this gospel suppresses the voice of one's conscience.

On the other end of the spectrum is the legalist. Like the libertines, legalists are the product of a certain kind of gospel. Legalists have a strong desire to please God. Their conversion to Christ has produced a change of values and lifestyle. They take God seriously, they take His Word seriously, and they try to honor Him in their conduct.

However, they have added a bundle of man-made rules to the Scriptures, and they tend to be judgmental toward those who fail to keep those rules. Yet they are intent on fulfilling the Christian standard; they may not always make it, but they'll die trying.

The gospel of legalism can be described as follows: God is holy, and He has made clear demands on the human race. We must warn, exhort, rebuke, and admonish ourselves and others to fulfill those demands. What follows is the language of the legalist:

> "You must …"
>
> "You need to …"
>
> "You have to …"
>
> "You had better …"
>
> "If you do … then God will be happy with you."
>
> "If you don't … then God will be angry with you."

The implication of such vocabulary is that if we fail to obey God's laws, then He will be displeased with us. Embedded in the gospel of legalism is the tacit threat that the Lord's love and acceptance of His children are tied to their conduct. This is rarely stated explicitly, but actions and behavior speak louder than words.

The gospel of legalism is aimed directly at the will. It gives human volition the illusion that it can keep the standards of God. At the same time, it weakens the conscience, causing it to believe that certain practices are sinful when they are not (1 Cor. 8; 10;

Rom. 14—15.) Theologian Alister McGrath rightly calls legalism "the dark side of evangelicalism."

There are obviously degrees of legalism, from mild to extreme, just as there are degrees of libertinism. I have probably described the extremes, but edit the descriptions slightly, and I believe you'll agree that the overwhelming majority of Christians can be put into one of these two camps.

Thankfully, there is a third gospel. Unfortunately, however, it's rarely preached today. This gospel is the one we find dominating the letters of Paul. It is the gospel of the new creation, if you will. It is neither libertine nor legalistic.

Instead of focusing on the demands of God, Paul's gospel focuses on the spiritual reality of what actually happens to those who have trusted in Christ when He died and rose again. It takes its view from behind the eyes of God—not from the earth but from the heavenlies.

Paul's gospel confidently proclaims that Jesus of Nazareth is this earth's true Lord. It declares the glories of Jesus and unflinchingly proclaims what God has done for all who submit to His lordship. The gospel that Paul preached includes salvation by grace through faith. It includes the call to repent, believe on Christ, and be baptized. It is a call to leave the world system and enter the kingdom of God—to move from the old fallen order into God's order. It includes the promise of the forgiveness of sins, eternal life, and the indwelling of the Holy Spirit.

In Paul's gospel, the standards of God are neither ignored nor rationalized into irrelevant oblivion (as in the gospel of the libertine). On the other hand, the standards of God are never presented as demands by which our acceptance by God is tied (as in the gospel of the legalist).

Contrary to the gospel of libertinism, Paul's gospel doesn't reduce faith to intellectual assent. (If you affirm the right propositions, you have "faith.")

Contrary to the gospel of legalism, Paul's gospel doesn't reduce good works to legalistic compliance. (If you perform these prescribed actions, you have "good works.")

Instead, Paul's gospel is rooted in the unconditional acceptance, security, and wealth that those who have trusted in Christ as Lord and Savior enjoy. For this reason, whenever Paul presents a standard of God, he always presents it from this vantage point: *It is the conduct that those who are in Christ naturally exhibit.*

In his epistles, Paul never teaches the standards of God as universal rules or laws to be obeyed. Rather, he mentions the Christian standard only when he is addressing a highly specific problem wherein God's people are not living according to who they are in Christ.

To the nonbeliever, Paul's gospel is aimed directly at the conscience. To the Christian, his gospel is aimed directly at the renewed spirit of humans, the new creation. Its message strengthens the spirit to take charge of the mind, the will, and the emotions. At the same time, it strengthens the conscience, causing it to be responsive to the Holy Spirit.

A crucial but little-accepted fact is that the New Testament is not a book of rules to regulate human behavior. Instead, the New Testament is a spiritual narrative made up of the following: history books that narrate the life of Jesus and the life of His church (the Gospels and Acts); personal letters to churches and individuals who are in crisis (the Epistles); and a majestic vision of Jesus Christ's triumphant victory over the world (Revelation).

Virtually all of Paul's letters were written in response to a particular crisis that God's people were experiencing. Remarkably, Paul's custom throughout his communications was to address the crisis in a first-second-third order:

First, he reminds God's people of their true identity in Christ. He also reminds them of the all-sufficiency of Christ who has come to dwell inside of them.

Second, he describes the behavior of those who are new creatures in Christ.

Third, he exhorts the believers to live according to their true identity rather than according to their false identity. That is, he exhorts them to walk in line with who they are in Christ rather than who they used to be in Adam.

Paul took this approach in virtually all of his epistles. It was his custom for addressing problems in the Christian communities under his care. The following statement from Ephesians is a perfect example of how Paul exhorts God's people to walk in a way that matches their high and holy calling:

> *For you were once darkness, but now you are light in the Lord. Live as children of light. (Eph. 5:8)*

In other words, you *are* light in Christ. Now *live* that way.

The gospel of libertinism, the gospel of legalism, and Paul's gospel represent three very different postures when it comes to matters of sin and morality. For the sake of illustration, let's take the issue of lying, which the New Testament condemns. (Feel free to insert any other sin that the Scriptures clearly address.)

Concerning the practice of lying, the libertine gospel essentially says, "This issue is irrelevant. We live in a different world than the people of the Bible did. Our values are different and more advanced. God loves us all and understands our needs. We all sin. Everybody lies. God loves everyone, so you are judging others if you tell them that they are wrong or immoral for lying."

The legalistic gospel says, "God will judge those who violate His commandments. Christians must not lie or else God will punish them."

In contrast, Paul's gospel exhorts, "Let me remind you that you are part of a new creation. Jesus Christ lives in you, and you are in Christ. As such, your old fallen nature is dead. Christ exterminated it by His cross. Therefore, put off the old lifestyle of lying. Such is the conduct of a fallen creation. It's not your conduct. Live according to who you really are and by the higher life that dwells within you. Jesus Christ is truth and honesty. Live out of what the Lord says you are ... for that alone is truth and reality."

Paul's gospel is built on the understanding that the key to spiritual transformation is not found in trying to improve oneself. It's found in being reminded again and again of who we are in Christ and who Christ is in us.

For Paul, the Christian life is becoming what you already are.

Our behavior as Christians stems from our identity. Consequently, the common approach Paul takes in his letters is to remind God's people of who they have become as new creatures in Christ. All of his exhortations flow out of that reminder.

The church of Jesus Christ is called to embody and proclaim the gospel that Paul preached—which is the gospel of Jesus Christ. That gospel is the good news of His kingdom coming and His will being done, that God is becoming ruler of the world He created and that Jesus, whom God the Father raised from the dead, is this world's true Lord.

Jesus Christ has defeated the powers of evil, sin, and death and has brought forth a new creation of which you are now a part. And one day, that new creation will fill the whole earth.

This is the full-hearted gospel, if you please; the others are impostors. Paul's gospel is one of liberty and lordship—the lordship of Christ and the liberty of the Spirit. It provides freedom from the fruitless attempt to keep a moral standard. It also provides freedom from the mastering power of the fallen nature.

Thus the Christian life is rooted in liberty—the liberty that is in Christ Jesus (Gal. 5:1). This is a liberty that sets us free from trying to be good. It is also a liberty that sets us free from practicing evil. It is a liberty that brings us into a living knowledge of the One who indwells us—the One who happens to be the greatest Liberator in the universe as well as the Savior and Lord of the world.

So the next time you hear someone preach or teach, ask yourself, "What gospel am I hearing? Am I being exhorted to feel comfortable in my sin and justify it (libertinism)? Am I being exhorted to try harder to be a better Christian (legalism)? Or am I being presented with my beautiful Savior, the Lord Jesus Christ, and reminded of my high standing in Him as a son or daughter of God (the gospel)?"

Embracing the gospel of libertinism or the gospel of legalism will tether you to the flesh. The fruit of libertinism is the defiling acts of the flesh. On another branch, but just as deadly, the fruit of legalism is the self-righteousness of the flesh.

Both gospels produce carnal activity and generate death rather than life. As a result, both clash with the new creation and have no place in the full-hearted gospel of Christ.

Only Paul's gospel—the glorious gospel of grace, the gospel of Jesus Christ—has the capacity to bring you and me into the freedom that is ours in Christ. And the end of that gospel is the ageless purpose of God for which our Lord burns.

Paul's Reminders[1]

The Pattern in Galatians

The truth is …

He has rescued you from this present evil age (1:4).

You have been justified by faith apart from the works of the law (2:16).

You have died to the law so that you may live to God. You have been crucified with Christ. You no longer live, but Christ lives in you. He loved you and gave Himself for you (2:19–20).

You received the Holy Spirit by believing (3:2).

You are children of Abraham (3:7).

Christ redeemed you from the curse of the law (3:13).

Since faith has come, you are no longer under the supervision of the law (3:25).

You are sons of God through faith in Jesus Christ. You were baptized in Christ, and you are clothed with Christ. You belong to Christ, and you are heirs to God's promise (3:26–29).

You are sons of God, and you have the full rights of sonship. Because you are sons, God has given you His Spirit. And that Spirit testifies that God is your Father. You are not slaves, but sons and heirs of God (4:4–7).

The heavenly Jerusalem is your mother (4:26).

You are children of promise (4:28).

You are called to be free (5:13).

You belong to Jesus Christ, and you have crucified the sinful nature with its passions and desires (5:24).

What counts is a new creation, of which you are a part (6:15).

Because of the above ...

Stand fast in the liberty that Christ has given you, and don't be burdened by the yoke of slavery to the law (5:1).

Do not use your freedom to indulge the sinful nature, but rather, serve one another in love (5:13).

Live by the Spirit, and you will not fulfill the desires of the sinful nature (5:16).

Since you live by the Spirit, keep in step with the Spirit. Do not be conceited, provoking and envying one another (5:25–26).

Carry one another's burdens (6:2).

Do not become weary in well-doing. Do good to all people, especially your fellow brethren in Christ (6:9–10).

The Pattern in 1 Corinthians

The truth is ...

You are holy in Christ, and you are called "holy ones" (1:2).

God's grace has been given to you in Christ. In Him, you have been enriched in every way. You do not lack any spiritual gift. He will keep you strong until the end so that you will be blameless on the day of Jesus Christ (1:4–8).

Because of God, you are in Christ Jesus who has become your wisdom, your righteousness, your holiness, and your redemption (1:30).

You have received the Spirit of God, not the spirit of the world, that you might know what God has freely given you (2:12).

You are God's temple, and God's Spirit lives in you (3:16).

Your body is the temple of the Holy Spirit who is in you. You are not your own. You were bought with a price (6:19–20).

Because of the above …

Be of the same mind, and have no divisions among you (1:10).

Since there are jealousy and quarreling among you, are you not worldly? Are you not acting like "mere men," contrary to who you really are? (3:3–4).

Do not deceive yourselves (3:18).

Judge nothing before the appointed time (4:5).

I urge you to imitate me (4:16).

Get rid of the old yeast among you, and expel the wicked man from among you (5:7, 13).

Flee from sexual immorality, and honor God with your body (6:18, 20).

The Pattern in Colossians

The truth is ...

You are holy and faithful in Christ (1:2).

The Father has qualified you to share in His inheritance. He has rescued you from the dominion of darkness. He has transferred you into the kingdom of Christ. In Christ, you have redemption and the forgiveness of sins (1:12–14).

He is the Head of His body, the church, of which you are a part (1:18).

Once you were enemies alienated from God. Now
He has reconciled you by Christ's death to present
you holy and blameless in His sight, without
blemish and free from accusation (1:21–22).

Christ is in you, the hope of glory (1:27).

You have received Christ Jesus as your Lord (2:6).

You have been given fullness in Christ. In Him,
you were spiritually circumcised and have put off
the sinful nature. You were buried with Christ by
baptism and have been raised with Him through
faith in the power of God who raised Him from the
dead (2:10–12).

God made you alive with Christ. He forgave you
of your sins. He canceled the written code that was
against you and opposed you. He nailed that code to
His cross (2:13–14).

You have died with Christ to the basic elements of
this world (2:20).

You have been raised with Christ (3:1).

You died, and your life is hidden with Christ in God. Christ is your life. When He appears, you will appear with Him (3:3–4).

You used to walk in the sinful nature. You have taken off the old self with its practices and put on the new self, which is being renewed in knowledge in the image of your Creator (3:7–10).

You are God's chosen people, holy and dearly loved (3:12).

You are members of one body and are called to peace (3:15).

Because of the above …

Continue to walk in Christ, just as you received Him (2:6).

See to it that no one takes you captive by deceptive philosophy that is not according to Christ (2:8).

Do not let anyone judge you in what you eat or drink or in regard to keeping a religious festival, a new moon celebration, or a Sabbath day (2:16).

Set your hearts on things above where Christ is seated at the right hand of God. Set your minds on things above, not on earthly things (3:1–2).

Put to death whatever belongs to your earthly nature (3:5).

Rid yourselves of such things as anger, rage, malice, slander, and filthy language. Do not lie to each other (3:8–9).

Clothe yourselves with compassion, kindness, humility, gentleness, and patience. Bear with each other, and forgive whatever grievances you have against one another. Forgive as the Lord forgave you. Put on love. Let the peace of Christ rule in your heart. Be thankful. Let the word of Christ dwell in you richly. Whatever you do, do it in the name of the Lord Jesus, giving thanks to God (3:12–17).

Devote yourselves to prayer, being watchful and thankful (4:2).

Let your conversation be always full of grace (4:6).

The Pattern in Ephesians

The truth is …

God has blessed you with all spiritual blessings in heavenly places in Christ. He chose you in Christ before the creation of the world so that you would be holy and blameless in His sight. In love, He predestined you to be adopted as His sons through Jesus Christ. He has freely given you His grace, and you are accepted in His Beloved Son. In Him you have redemption through His blood, the forgiveness of sins. He has lavished the riches of His grace upon you with all wisdom and understanding (1:3–8).

In Christ, you were chosen and predestined according to His eternal plan. You have been given an inheritance in Him (1:11).

You were included in Christ. You were marked in
Him with a seal of the promised Holy Spirit. The
Spirit is a deposit guaranteeing your inheritance. You
are God's possession (1:13–14).

You used to be dead in your trespasses and sins. You
used to follow the way of the world and the ruler of
the kingdom of darkness (2:1–2).

God, who has a great love for you and who is rich
in mercy, made you alive in Christ, even when
you were dead in transgressions. You have been
saved by grace. God raised you up with Christ and
seated you with Him in the heavenly realms in
Christ Jesus in order that in the coming ages He
might show the incomparable riches of His grace,
expressed in His kindness to you in Christ Jesus.
You have been saved by grace, through faith. It is
not of yourselves, but it is the gift of God. Not by
works, lest any person should boast. You are God's
workmanship created in Christ Jesus to do good
works, which God prepared in advance for you to
do (2:4–10).

You are now in Christ Jesus. You were once far away, but you have been brought near by the blood of Christ (2:13).

He Himself is your peace (2:14).

Through Christ you have access to the Father by one Spirit (2:18).

You are fellow citizens with God's people and members of God's household (2:19).

You are being built together to become a dwelling place in which God lives by His Spirit (2:22).

You are members of one body (4:25).

You are dearly loved children (5:1).

Christ loved you and gave Himself up for you as a fragrant offering and sacrifice to God (5:2).

You are God's holy people (5:3).

For you were once darkness, but now you are light in
the Lord (5:8).

Because of the above ...

I urge you to live a life worthy of the calling you
have received. Be completely humble and gentle;
be patient, bearing with one another in love. Make
every effort to keep the unity of the Spirit through
the bond of peace (4:1–3).

You must no longer live as the Gentiles do, in the
futility of their thinking. You didn't come to learn
Christ that way. You were taught to put away your old
self, to be made new in the attitude of your minds,
and to put on the new self, created to be like God in
true righteousness and holiness. Therefore, each of
you must put off falsehood and speak truthfully to his
neighbor. In your anger do not sin. He who has been
stealing must steal no longer but must work. Do not
let any unwholesome word come out of your mouth,
but only what is helpful for the building up of others
according to their needs. Do not grieve the Holy Spirit.
Get rid of all bitterness, rage and anger, brawling and

slander, along with every form of malice. Be kind and compassionate to one another, forgiving each other, just as Christ has forgiven you (4:17, 20–32).

Be imitators of God, and live a life of love (5:1–2).

There must not be sexual immorality, impurity, greed, obscenity, foolish talk, or coarse jesting among you, which are out of place, but rather thanksgiving (5:3–4).

Do not be partners with those who practice these things (5:7).

Have nothing to do with the fruitless deeds of darkness, but rather expose them (5:11).

Do not get drunk on wine, which leads to debauchery. Instead, be filled with the Spirit. Speak to one another in psalms, hymns, and spiritual songs. Sing and make music in your heart to the Lord. Always give thanks to God. Submit to one another out of reverence for Christ (5:18–21).

Acknowledgments

I'd like to thank John Blase for the title of this book and Alan Hirsch for giving me the language of "rescripting." I also owe a debt to my friends Hal Miller, Frank Valdez, and Jon Zens for inspiring some of the content.

Notes

Chapter 1: God's Three-Fold Speaking

1. This list owes much to Gary Holt's essay "Hermeneutics in Everyday Life."

2. Some New Testament scholars believe that a lost document called "Q" was the source for some of the material in the gospels of Matthew and Luke.

3. I owe my awareness of these texts to Walter Brueggemann in an essay of his that I read many years ago.

Chapter 3: Let Me Pray About It

1. I've addressed this issue extensively in my eBook *Rethinking the Will of God*, www.ptmin.org/rethinkingthewill.pdf.

Chapter 4: Spiritual Conversational Styles

1. This chapter owes a great deal to my friend Hal Miller and Deborah Tannen, author of *That's Not What I Meant!*

2. There's a close connection between a person's SCS and the three modes in which God communicates His mind (see chapter 1). Typically, the Charismatic recognizes God speaking only through the prophetic, the Quoter recognizes God speaking only through Torah, and the Pragmatic recognizes God speaking only through wisdom.

Chapter 5: What's Wrong with Our Gospel?

1. See *Jesus Manifesto* coauthored with Leonard Sweet.

2. By "Christian life" I mean the life that Jesus lived, which was a lifestyle lived by His Father's life. And it served as an example for all Christians (followers of Jesus).

3. See my book *From Eternity to Here* for a detailed discussion on the eternal purpose of God.

4. Voices of the Innovators, "The Seed of Apple's Innovation," *BusinessWeek*, October 12, 2004, www.businessweek.com/bwdaily/dnflash/oct2004/nf20041012_4018_db083.htm (accessed February 4, 2010).

5. Obviously, God the Father and the Holy Spirit do not wear out either. But all of the fullness of the Godhead dwells in Jesus, and we come to know the Father by the Spirit through Christ.

Chapter 7: Captured by the Same Spirit You Oppose

1. Saint John of the Cross, *The Living Flame of Love* (New York: Cosimo, 2007), 76.

2. For a fuller treatment on the cancer of self-righteousness and how the Lord views it, see chapter 8 of *From Eternity to Here*.

Chapter 9: Stripping Down to Christ Alone

1. Rob McAlpine, *Post-Charismatic?* (Eastbourne, UK: Kingsway, 2008).

2. A tendency to exaggerate the miraculous and go to emotional extremes appeared at the very inception of the movement. See Frank Bartleman's book *Another Wave of Revival.*

3. Frank Bartleman, *Another Wave of Revival* (Springdale, PA: Whitaker, 1982), 94–96.

Chapter 10: Your Christ Is Too Small

1. To read more about what it means to pursue Jesus corporately, see my book *Reimagining Church*.

2. This is what the Greek text says. See Leon Morris, *The Gospel According to John* (Grand Rapids, MI: Eerdmans, 1995), 741–43.

3. For details, see my book *The Untold Story of the New Testament Church*.

Afterword: The Three Gospels

1. These biblical-book patterns are organized chronologically—not by order of appearance in the New Testament. Also, Scripture passages in this section are paraphrased.

About the Author

FRANK VIOLA is a frequent conference speaker and author of numerous books on the deeper Christian life and radical church restoration. His books include the best-selling *From Eternity to Here* along with *Pagan Christianity* (coauthored with George Barna), *Reimagining Church, Finding Organic Church, Jesus Manifesto* (coauthored with Leonard Sweet), and *The Untold Story of the New Testament Church*. Frank's Web site, www.FrankViola.com, contains many free resources, including audio messages, an interactive blog, a quarterly eNewsletter, articles, and more. Frank and his family live in Gainesville, Florida.

"Who do you say that I am?"

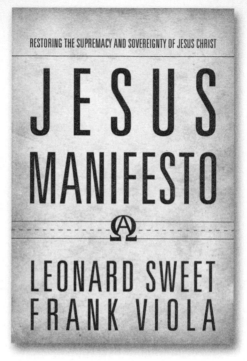

RESTORING THE SUPREMACY AND SOVEREIGNTY OF JESUS CHRIST

JESUS MANIFESTO

LEONARD SWEET
FRANK VIOLA

Jesus Manifesto presents a fresh unveiling of Jesus as not only Savior and Lord, but as so much more.

It is a prophetic call to restore the supremacy and sovereignty of Christ in a world—and a church—that has lost sight of Him.

Every revival and restoration in the church has been a rediscovery of some aspect of Christ in the process of answering the ultimate question that Jesus put to His disciples.

Read this book and see your Lord like you've never seen Him before.

- -

THOMAS NELSON
Since 1798

Available wherever books and e-books are sold!